JOHN ROSEMOND'S FAIL-SAFE FORMULA FOR HELPING YOUR CHILD SUCCEED IN SCHOOL

JOHN ROSEMOND

Andrews McMeel Publishing

Kansas City • Sydney • London

To my seven grandchildren: Jack, Patrick, Thomas (a.k.a. Rodney),
James, Connor, Anna Caitlin, and Holden

ACKNOWLEDGMENT AND DEDICATION

John Donne wrote, "No man is an island." Indeed, no one who has ever written a book can claim complete credit.

I've spent my career—more than forty years at this writing—working with parents, teachers, and children concerning developmental, behavioral, and academic issues. In the process, I've learned much more than I could possibly have learned if I'd spent that time in graduate school.

Then there are my own children, Eric and Amy, now adults with children of their own. They taught me that children do much better in school without parents breathing down their necks, checking their homework, and sitting with them when they do it, providing benevolent but counterproductive "help." Today, most parents have been seduced by the "good parents get involved" mantra that started in the 1970s. Maybe I'm just fundamentally lazy, but where school was concerned, Willie and I told the kids that their job was to make sure we never had to get involved. They figured out rather quickly how to do exactly that. Pretty much on their own, they did well enough academically to get into good colleges and make very good grades. And by the way, it seems Willie and I are the only parents in the United States who were never gifted with a "gifted" child.

Willie deserves more than a mention, for sure. She has learned to wait patiently for my company while I am writing a book. That can't be an easy thing for any author's spouse, but she does it well. She is why I meet my deadlines. Because I had already moved on to writing another book, Willie went through the page proofs for this one with the proverbial fine-toothed comb, making necessary corrections. Thanks, Babes. Love you; mean it.

Numerous researchers, unbeknownst to them, contributed to this book. Lots of people in my field are inclined to making things up. They seem to think that since Sigmund Freud became famous for the stuff he made up, they're simply carrying on a well-established psychological tradition. I make a conscious effort to be sure that everything I say publicly is backed by solid research. In the process, I've discovered that good research in psychology always, without any exception I've run across, confirms common sense.

Finally, there's the folks at Andrews McMeel in Kansas City, especially my faithful editor, Christine Schillig, who put the final touches on the manuscript, thus making me sound like a much better writer than I am.

CONTENTS

Love Is Always Lovelier the Second Time Around

In 1990, Andrews McMeel published the first version of this book, titled *Ending the Homework Hassle*. It did quite well, in every sense of the term. It sold extremely well, more than enough for me to make back my advance and then some, which is every author's immediate goal. Best of all, it accomplished my purpose. Over the years, many parents have told me the book helped them solve major school performance and classroom behavior problems. That means it also helped children become happier little people. Educators liked it too. A good number of schools made it required reading for their teachers, many of whom told me they often recommended it to parents.

As the title implies, that first version focused largely on homework management. At the time, schools were beginning to embrace the entirely imprudent notion that parental involvement in homework would pay off in higher achievement. I knew that wasn't and wouldn't be the case and said so several times in my syndicated newspaper column. Nonetheless, schools pressed on, pressuring parents to help their kids with homework, study for tests, and partner with them on science projects. It certainly caught on. Today, it is the rare parent who is not involved in her child's homework, making sure it gets done and back to school without error. The use of the female pronoun in that sentence was deliberate. I would guess that mothers make up 95 percent of adult homework helpers.

And sure enough, my prediction has proven correct. As parent involvement in homework has increased, student achievement across the demographic spectrum has declined. There is no empirical evidence that this very dysfunctional practice is bearing anything but rotten fruit. Although the people who encouraged and still encourage it have college degrees, it does not take a college degree to understand why adult participation in homework is counterproductive.

- First, a child who knows his mother is prepared to reteach the material at home is incentivized to *not* pay attention in class. In effect, the child exchanges paying attention in class for his mother's one-on-one attention at home. Furthermore, the less he pays attention in class, the more of his mother's attention he receives. Common sense will tell you this is a counterproductive arrangement and that the child in question is gifted with an amazing ability to grasp interpersonal dynamics.

- Second, when responsibility for homework is shared, the child does not feel ownership of the work and therefore does not feel the need to put forth much effort. Shared responsibility means the benefit to the child is much lower.

- Third, the adult ends up being an enabler, doing things for the child that the child is capable of doing for himself. No matter the context or issue, enabling weakens the skill-set of the person being enabled—always.

- Fourth, the more the mother enables, the more she identifies with and personalizes her child's school performance— grades, especially—which means that his grades become *her* grades, making it all but inevitable that she will complain when a grade is not what she thought it should be.

Now, if one reasonably smart guy—yours truly—can figure that out, why hasn't anyone in America's vast education establishment come to the same conclusion? Because despite a complete lack of evidence that parent participation in homework is working and an abundance of evidence to the commonsensical effect that it is *not* working, schools continue to recommend that parents get involved in their children's homework. In psychological terms, America's schools—public and private—are in *denial* about this issue. The evidence is staring them in the face, and they refuse to acknowledge it. Such is the nature of bureaucracies. Once a bunch of bureaucrats decides that something should be done a certain way and that way becomes standard practice but consistently fails to generate positive outcomes, it can take the proverbial (and sometimes literal) act of Congress for the bureaucrats to decide that the thing should not be done any longer. America's education establishment has been cheerleading for parent participation in homework since the 1970s and is not about to admit it isn't working. At this point, the education bureaucracy is not about to yield to the evidence that's staring them in the face.

Time has proved me right, and so I continue to encourage parents to stay a safe distance from their children's homework. And by the way, I have *never* had a parent tell me that she followed my homework management plan as described in Chapter 3 and her child suffered permanent academic collapse. Quite the contrary, parents tell me that after an inevitable but temporary period of adjustment on the child's part (during which time the child's performance may go slightly downhill), the child begins doing better than ever in school. More than one mom has told me, tongue in cheek, "Your book saved my child's life, John." Did I mention that parent participation in homework can drive a parent to the brink of filicide?

A few years after writing *Ending the Homework Hassle*, I began to wish I could rewrite certain portions. I'd learned a lot in the interim, and even though parents and teachers continued to give the book high marks, my personal dissatisfaction was growing. By the turn of the new millennium, I was telling people to skip over the chapter on "When to Medicate." I had come to the reluctant conclusion that there was no credible science behind the diagnosis of attention deficit–hyperactivity disorder (ADHD). The claims made by professionals who specialized in the diagnosis and "treatment" of ADHD were and are bogus. The diagnosis was and is bogus. The so-called treatments were and are bogus. There was no compelling evidence that the cluster of behaviors being called ADHD were inherited, that they had anything to do with biochemical imbalances or brain differences, or that the medications being given to these unfortunate kids were anything more than expensive placebos, with one exception: Placebos don't have dangerous side effects. My research led me to form a relationship with an outlier pediatrician, DuBose Ravenel, and he and I eventually wrote a book exposing the ADHD fraud: *The Diseasing of America's Children*. The long and short of it is that I've written a new chapter on this incendiary issue. It's still titled "When to Medicate," the answer being *never*. Once you've read the chapter and if you have a continuing interest in the subject, you'll find a great deal more information in *The Diseasing of America's Children*.

I've whacked a bunch of material from *Ending the Homework Hassle*, but I've added a lot as well, including a chapter on homeschooling. I'm a fan of homeschooling. If my wife and I had it to do all over again, we would homeschool our kids all the way through high school. I'm a regular speaker at homeschool conferences, and I talk with lots of homeschooling parents. For several years, I served on the board of parentalrights.org, which spun off from the Home School Legal Defense Association. In the process of this semi-immersion in homeschool culture, I've come to the conclusion that most homeschool moms have bought right into the prevailing parent involvement myth.

"But John," hundreds of homeschooling moms have said to me, "I homeschool—I *have* to be highly involved, don't I?"

My answer to that question is in Chapter 8. Don't want to ruin it for you.

I've also greatly expanded the Q&A section at the end of each chapter.

So for all those reasons, I felt that a new title was appropriate for this rewrite: *John Rosemond's Fail-Safe Formula for Helping Your Child Succeed in School.*

I sincerely hope this book will be even more helpful to more parents (and therefore children) than was the original version. It ought to be. I'm older, wiser, and generally much improved over the John Rosemond I was in 1990. Aging can do that to you—*should,* in fact.

Building Strong Foundations

During a child's preschool years a template forms that will determine the level of success the child experiences in school. The features that make up this template include the child's brain development, attention span, respect for authority, imagination, creativity, enthusiasm for learning, and self-image. The integrity and functionality of this template will determine whether the child realizes his or her academic potential. Over the course of my career—at this writing, forty-plus years in the making—I've consulted with hundreds of schools, spoken to and consulted with thousands of teachers, administered batteries of tests to hundreds of children, and advised thousands of parents on all manner of parenting concerns, including the full gamut of academic issues. In the process, I've personally encountered or heard about lots of kids with high IQs who were not doing well in school. They don't pay attention in class, don't finish work, are burdened by numerous behavior problems, lack respect for authority figures, and in many cases just don't seem to care. They take no personal pride in good grades. Many of these children qualify as "gifted," meaning their IQs are above 130. Unfortunately, many of them also qualify as brats.

On the other hand, I've met and been told about many kids whose IQs were in the average range (90 to 110) but who were enthusiastic about learning and highly motivated to always do their best. Kids who fit this description behave properly in class, follow school rules, participate in class discussions, play well with other children, are respectful to the teacher and classmates, do their class-work and homework without having to be artificially motivated in one way or another, and always do their best. They may not make top grades, but teachers never fail to identify them as their best students.

Intelligence is certainly part of the picture of a child's school performance, but it is not the most important variable. Playing Mozart to your child while he's in utero, hiring a tutor to teach him a foreign language when he's three years old, purchasing expensive toys that supposedly promote the growth of specific brain structures—those things may pay off in terms of high grades, inclusion in gifted and talented programs, and college scholarships. On the other hand, they may not. The things that seem to matter most to a child's success in school are surprising to many people. They might even surprise a good number of educators.

Marriage Matters

I'll just bet that if I asked one hundred parents, "What do you think is the single best thing you can do to help your child succeed in school?" not *one* of them would give the correct answer. Some would say teaching reading and math facts during the preschool years. Other answers would include choosing the best schools possible, teaching a second language, parent involvement, helping with homework, modeling the value of reading at home, keeping television and other screen time to a minimum, and reading to the child from infancy on. Most of those practices are important to varying degrees, but some, like teaching reading and math facts before kindergarten, aren't important at all (more on that startling fact later). Believe it or not, the best thing parents can do to ensure a child's success in school, regardless of the child's IQ or the family's demographics, is for the parents to have a good marriage.

That is not simply my opinion. That's the finding of an increasing body of research in the social sciences and on early brain development. Some of that research is coming out of Seattle's Telaris Research Institute, which works with scientists and educators to translate findings in early brain development into practical advice for parents. Bioengineering expert John Medina, Telaris's founding director, says, "The best evidence we have suggests that one of the best predictors of cognitive success is . . . not buying your baby a mobile; it's not even getting them to speak French by the age of one and a half. It actually has to do with the emotional stability of the home environment."

As politically incorrect as it may be, it's becoming increasingly clear that marriage provides the optimal emotionally stable home environment. Linda Waite, professor of sociology at the University of Chicago and co-author of *The Case for Marriage*, has found that children raised in two-married-parent homes do better in school and are more likely to graduate from college and enjoy satisfactory, productive adulthoods. Other investigators have discovered that just being raised in a married-parent household isn't enough. Rather, the *quality* of the husband–wife relationship is what really matters: The better the marriage, the better the child's chance of success academically, emotionally, socially, and later on in his or her chosen profession. Even more amazing is the finding that children raised by parents who are deeply in love with one another are smarter! The emotional stability their parents provide actually accelerates the healthy growth of their brains!

It appears that from day one a child's brain is responding to emotional cues coming from his parents. It's not enough that they love him; they need to be *in love* with one another. That means creating what I've long advocated through my books, weekly newspaper column, and public presentations: a marriage-centered home. Simply put, this is a home in which parents pay more attention to and even show more interest in one another than they do their kids. Granted, children need lots of parental attention during infancy and early toddlerhood, but it's equally the case that children need parents who pay lots of attention to each other. A marriage-centered family is one in which parents talk with one another more than they talk with their children, frequently embrace and kiss one another in front of the kids, go on an occasional adults-only weekend (or longer) romantic getaways, and spend a good amount of time just cuddling. The parents I'm talking about create lots of high-quality experiences for themselves and their families rather than letting children's activities consume nearly all the family's discretionary time.

The research just confirms what is common sense: Nothing ensures a child's sense of well-being—his feeling of emotional security and belonging—more than the knowledge that his parents are in a committed relationship with one another. Said another way, what matters most to your child is not the quality of your parenting but the quality of your marriage.

So forget about playing Mozart to your child when he's in the womb, toss out the preschool math flash cards, and stop buying expensive toys that supposedly increase left temporal lobe growth. Take the money you save and go on a second honeymoon to Tahiti—without the kids, of course.

Not for Single Parents Only

So what does this mean for a child raised in a single-parent home? Is he doomed to failure? Not at all. When considering research results, one must keep in mind that researchers report averages, not individual outcomes. In this case, they are finding that *on average* children raised in emotionally functional two-married-parent homes fare better than children raised in single-parent homes or homes that are marred by dysfunctional marriages. That does not mean that *every* child raised under those latter circumstances is going to have unsatisfactory school and life experiences. There are plenty of exceptions to any research-based average. I'm one. I was raised by a single mother for most of the first seven years of my life. My father visited with me once, for part of a day, when I was five. I didn't see him again for four years and infrequently from that point on. And my mother and stepfather were definitely not in love with one another. They were in constant and sometimes downright scary conflict. But despite the obvious shortcomings, my early childhood experience wasn't a big negative. In fact, I think that growing up in a single-parent household has helped me understand single parenthood from a child's point of view. Specifically, my early years with a mother who worked, went to college, and had a full social life have caused me to appreciate how essential it is—for both parent and child—that single parents create lives that bring them a full measure of emotional satisfaction. By the way, that is precisely what the research into divorce finds: The well-being of a child of divorced parents is predicted largely by the well-being of the primary custodial parent. My mother did a good job during my early years—for herself and me both.

Whenever a single mother asks my advice, I always point out that in addition to providing a loving home environment and disciplining properly, she has two important obligations to her children:

- First, she must demonstrate through her own example that *women are interesting people*. She won't be able to do that if she overfocuses on her children so they come to regard her as a human vending machine, someone who is there simply to dispense goodies. She accomplishes this by living a life in which the role of mother is a part-time job—an important job, of course, but not one that consumes her body and soul. She needs to have interests and pursuits separate and apart from her parental responsibilities. Entirely too many single and married women make motherhood a full time, 24/7/365 job and lose a full, complete, healthy sense of their own identities in the process.

- Second, she should prove to her children that *authority resides legitimately in women*. She accomplishes this by exercising proper—meaning firm, resolute, and loving—authority over her kids. For more on this, I recommend my book *The Well-Behaved Child: Discipline That Really Works!*

Would it have been better for me if I'd been raised by two parents who were in love with one another? Absolutely, but the fact that a loving parental marriage was not in the cards for me did not leave emotional scars. It left *gaps* that as an adult, in order to become a good husband and father, I had to acknowledge and figure out how to fill. But then, no matter how ideal a child's life may be, one always grows up with gaps. Such is life. I often remind myself that by virtue of the fact that I grew up in America, I got a better start in life than 75 percent of the world's kids—despite the less-than-ideal circumstances in which I was raised.

By the way, in case someone finds it relevant, I was a straight-A student. But then, I grew up with three distinct advantages: First, I had a mother whose authority was calmly communicated and yet unquestionable; second, there was no television (until I was eleven), computers, cell phones, or video games; and third, I did chores from the time I was three years old. In short, despite the lack of two parents for most of my first seven years, I was blessed with an otherwise normal early childhood, one that prepared me for paying attention in class, doing the work my teachers assigned, and doing my best (most of the time—after all, I was a boy).

A Brief Word on School Reform

Whenever I speak on the subject of success in school to a group of educators, parents, or both, I tell them that I don't believe in school reform. We began trying to reform America's schools in the 1960s. Before then, the schools worked. In the 1950s, the high school graduation rate was around 82 percent. It is now around 68 percent. During the same period, the functional literacy rate of sixteen-year-olds has declined commensurate with a drastic decline in academic standards. It is now possible for a youngster to obtain a valid high school diploma at age eighteen or nineteen but be reading with comprehension at only a fifth-grade level. Respect for authority has declined since schools embraced the notion that teachers should try to be liked by their students. I could go on, but I think I've proved my point: No post-1950s attempt to reform America's schools has worked. Furthermore, I don't think there is a magic school reform that is going to set things right again. For all these reasons, I don't believe in school reform. If positive change is going to happen in America's schools, it will happen because of home reform. It will happen because parents step up to the plate and create conditions in their homes that promote intellectual curiosity, creativity, responsibility, and perhaps most importantly, respect for adult authority. It will happen because parents place much greater value on reading than watching television. It will happen because parents give permission to teachers to discipline and they support teachers when children complain that they have been disciplined at school. *Home* reform, not school reform, is the key to America regaining the world lead in education. To paraphrase the refrain of a popular song, America's schools have been looking for love in all the wrong places.

Home Reform, Part 1: Respect for Authority

In order for someone to learn something from someone else, that person must look up to the other one. Without respect and admiration for a teacher's knowledge and authority, the student will not maximize his learning potential. He will not pay the teacher adequate attention, follow directions properly, or put forth his best effort. No matter what his IQ, he will not be a good student. In all likelihood, he will also bring behavior problems with him to school that further interfere with his ability to put his intelligence to good use. He may eventually become diagnosed with a learning disability or childhood behavior disorder of one sort or another.

As he progresses through the grades, his attitude toward his teachers and the educational process as a whole may become increasingly cynical. His inability to derive the full value of his academic education may even lead him to drop out of school as soon as he is able; and yes, even some very intelligent kids drop out of school. Regardless, he'll probably drop out mentally sometime around junior high school. When he enters adult society, his disdain for authority will cause him untold problems throughout his life.

In the simplest, most accurate terms, a good student pays attention in class, does what his teachers tell him to do, and does his best at all times. He is respectful, obedient, and responsible. Those attributes are formed at home by loving parents who discipline properly.

Because of their unconditional love, their children want to please them. Because they discipline properly, their children rise to their expectations. Therefore, the children bring a desire to please and self-motivation to school and transfer it to their teachers.

When I speak to teacher groups, I conduct a poll that illustrates the importance of this home training. I ask teachers to tell me whether they'd rather teach a classroom full of children who all (a) have IQs above 150 but are inattentive and difficult to motivate or (b) possess normal intelligence (IQs of 90 to 110) but are attentive and self-motivated. That's a no-brainer for teachers. No teacher has ever said she would rather teach the inattentive geniuses. In other words, the good student is not defined in terms of how smart he or she is. The good student is, in a word, *respectful*. He pays attention in class, follows instructions, obeys the rules, is eager to please the teachers, does his best, participates in class discussions, looks for ways of doing more than just the minimum, and, for all those reasons, learns, learns, learns.

It is essential that parents teach their children to be respectful of adults, and that lesson definitely begins in the home, with respect for one's parents. Teaching respect requires that parents clearly occupy the center of the family. A two-parent family should be marriage-centered: The parents should be in much more of a relationship with one another than they are with their kids. A single-parent family should be parent-centered: The single parent must, for her children's sake as well as her own, make sure she lives a well-rounded life that her children find interesting. If this sounds heretical, as if I'm advocating some subtle form of neglect, it's only because many people have been seduced by the children-come-first mentality that our society (and a good number of parenting experts) promote.

Whether presided over by a single parent or two parents, a family should be centered by the adult presence, and children should orbit around that star. This state of affairs helps children divest themselves of self-centeredness, which is essential to developing a respectful attitude toward adults. It also says to the children, "You are expected to pay attention to us."

You *do* want your children to pay attention to you, don't you? Then you *must* occupy the central, most prominent position in your family. You cannot expect your children to pay attention to you if you act, day in and day out, as if your most pressing obligation is that of paying attention to *them.*

Here's a simple, incontrovertible fact: *The more attention parents pay a child, the less attention the child will pay the parents.*

By his or her third birthday, a child understands that it is either his job to pay attention to his parents or their job to pay attention to and do things for him. Those two understandings are mutually exclusive. They do not coexist. And by the way, from age three on, whether the child is easy to discipline (well-behaved) or difficult to discipline (ill-behaved) largely depends on whether he does or does not pay sufficient attention to his parents. The "whether or not" depends entirely on them and how effectively they communicate their authority.

The unwritten understanding between parent and child should be, "When I, your parent, want your attention, you have no choice other than to pay attention to me. However, when you want attention from me, I will decide whether it is prudent and necessary to give that attention to you at that time." In other words, the parent has a choice; the child does not. Furthermore, the mere fact that a child *wants* attention does not mean he should receive it. Children often want what they do not need and should find out, as early in life as possible, that Mick Jagger was correct when he said, "You can't always get what you want, but if you try sometimes you just might find you get what you need."

Unfortunately, in many families this fundamental understanding has been turned upside-down and inside-out. Many parents act as if they are obligated to pay attention to their children whenever their children want it, and especially if they demand it or ask for it with pitiful expressions on their faces. Today's parents seem to believe that if they deny their children attention, they will make the children insecure or induce some other psychological malfunction. This belief was handed down from on high by a number of so-called experts who wrote books about child rearing, and it has since become solidly entrenched in our culture.

The myth is that children need a lot of attention, and that the more attention you pay a child, the more you inflate his sense of self-esteem. The truth, in three parts:

- Infants need a lot of attention, toddlers need a lot of supervision, and children need less and less of either as they grow past toddlerhood.

- Children have great difficulty distinguishing need from want. They often want what they do not need and, equally often, need what they do not want. Parents' responsibilities include helping their children come to grips with that difference. People who do not come to grips with it are destined for all manner of difficulty in life. They are perpetually frustrated, disgruntled malcontents. In effect, they've never grown up. You know adults who fit this description, don't you? And I'm sure you don't want your child to become that sort of adult.

- The idea that it's a good thing for a person to possess high self-esteem—the feeling that one is "special" and can reach any goal he wants to reach—is also a myth. According to the latest and best research, high self-esteem is associated with lack of respect for others, lack of good emotional coping skills, and an entitlement mentality.

Yes, high self-esteem is not a desirable attribute. So says the research—*all* of it. Your job is to properly prepare your children for good citizenship, and the research is clear that high self-esteem is not conducive to being a good neighbor. Good citizenship is all about responsibility, service to others, doing one's best at all times, and personal modesty. It appears that people with high opinions of themselves are generally lacking in all of those attributes. Instead of respecting others, they *expect* from others. Furthermore, when someone with high self-esteem doesn't get what he wants from someone else, he's likely to become downright mean, even aggressive. For example, it has been found that spouse abusers have very high self-esteem. And if life doesn't deal the cards he expects to someone with high self-esteem, he's likely to become despondent, depressed. This is not the sort of adulthood you want for your children.

Whenever I discuss what social scientists are now saying about high self-esteem, people begin to experience what psychologists call cognitive dissonance. Since the term *self-esteem* was introduced into the vernacular in the late 1960s, Americans have come to take its value for granted. So my reportage of the cold, hard facts causes confusion. People often ask this question: "But if I don't want my child to have high self-esteem, do I want him to have *low* self-esteem?" I answer that no, you want him to have a realistic view of himself. He should clearly understand that he is a person with both strengths and weaknesses (people with high self-esteem have great difficulty thinking of themselves as having any weaknesses at all) and that he is capable of being a *useful* adult (and that usefulness is not measured by income).

Another way of looking at this is to say that people with high self-esteem expect rewards regardless of performance, whereas a feeling of capability, of self-worth, is its own reward. People with high self-esteem are motivated by external rewards; they're needy. People who possess feelings of self-worth are motivated intrinsically. They accomplish whatever they accomplish for the self-reward (the sense of self-satisfaction) that naturally accompanies accomplishment; to them, extrinsic rewards are secondary.

Home Reform, Part 2:
Usefulness and Family Citizenship

School is a responsible environment. To the degree that children come to school primed with and for responsibility, they will accept the functions expected of them by their teachers. A teacher cannot instill a sense of responsibility in a child; she can only capitalize on what is already there.

The most effective means of priming a child for responsibility is to promote good family citizenship. And the way to do that is to assign a regular, daily routine of chores around the home. The time to begin assigning chores is shortly after a child's third birthday. At first, a child should be responsible simply for picking up his toys, keeping his room orderly, and clearing his own plate and silverware from the table. As he grows, his duties should extend into common areas of the home. By the time a child is of kindergarten age, he or she should be practiced at sweeping, dusting, running a vacuum cleaner, taking out garbage, setting and clearing the table, helping with the washing and drying of dishes, and making his own bed. Outdoors, a five-year-old is fully capable of helping with raking, sweeping, weeding, and watering. If that seems incredible, it's only because we have forgotten that in the 1950s, most of America's five-year-olds were doing those very sorts of things routinely.

Chores are important because they are a child's only means of making a tangible contribution to the family. Performed on a regular basis, these acts

- ◆ Bond a child to the family and its values. For proof of this, ask yourself, "Where in America have family values and traditions been handed down most stably and reliably from generation to generation?" The answer is in rural areas where, not coincidentally, it is normal for children to participate in the work of their families from an early age.

- Actualize the child's membership in the family. All acts of contribution are acts of participation. To the extent the child participates in the life of the family, his membership is acknowledged and affirmed. That affirmation imparts a sense of security to the child that cannot come as well from any other source.

- Give the child a sense of usefulness and worth. Chores are a means of accomplishment for a child. Every opportunity for accomplishment is an opportunity to develop the intrinsic reward of a sense of usefulness (also known as self-worth).

- At the most practical level, chores teach important domestic skills. Your child's spouse will someday thank you for that.

- Prepare children for good citizenship. President John F. Kennedy gave Americans the perfect prescription for responsible citizenship when he said, "Ask not what your country can do for you; ask what you can do for your country." For a child to eventually become a good citizen of this country, he must first be a good citizen of his family. To accomplish this, parents must teach their children that it is better to seek ways of doing for the family than to expect the family to constantly do for them.

Considering all of the above, there is absolutely no excuse for not expecting children to perform a daily routine of chores in and around the home. Unfortunately, there are many more American children who do *not* contribute to their families on a regular basis than there are children who do. Parents rationalize this failure in a number of ways. Here are the top four:

- "It's more of a hassle to get the kids to do something around the house and do it right than it is for us to do it ourselves." This is a cop-out of the first magnitude.

- ◆ "What with all the after-school activities they're involved in, there's no time for our children to do much work around the house." This is a cop-out of the second magnitude.
- ◆ "We believe childhood should be a relaxed, carefree time, not filled with responsibilities. We think that expecting them to do well in school is enough." This is a cop-out of the third magnitude.
- ◆ "There really isn't that much for the children to do around the house because we have both a cleaning service and a yard service that come in once a week." This is a cop-out of the fourth magnitude.

First, it is indeed worth the hassle, which will be short-lived if parents simply take a stand on the subject of chores and stand firm. Second, if a child is involved in so many after-school activities that he has no time to do chores, then he's involved in too many after-school activities. It's a simple matter of priorities—first things first. Third, a child who is responsible around the home will be more responsible at school. He will be a better all-around student because he will bring to school a stronger desire for accomplishment. So do your children a favor and save yourself some money by letting the cleaning service and the yard service go!

In his or her family, a child is either a consumer or a *contributing* consumer. If the former, through no fault of his own the child is in a position of poor family citizenship. "You can get something for nothing" is the powerful message sent to a child who is not a fully participating member of his or her family. The idea that something can be had for nothing is a falsehood, but a child who has lived within the fantasy that's implicit in that falsehood is very likely to bring that fantasy to school. He is likely to believe that education, like everything else that's ever come his way, is something someone *gives* you. Of course, that isn't true. Education is something you *get* for yourself. Someone may extend the opportunity to you, but whether you take advantage of it or not is strictly a matter of choice. How do you want your child to choose?

The child who is not a contributing consumer, a good family citizen, is likely to bring an entitlement attitude to the workplace when he becomes an adult. Given the number of chore-free kids in America, it should come as no surprise that managers often use the words *entitled* and *entitlement* to describe many young employees.

One such manager told me, "All too many of today's college graduates aren't looking for jobs, John; they're looking for benefits. They expect their employers to continue the entitlements their parents accustomed them to."

This could well have a negative impact on America's economic standing in the world unless American parents wake up and smell the proverbial coffee. I know that young people in China, India, Indonesia, Malaysia, and South Korea—emerging economic powerhouses—are not entering the workplace with an entitlement mentality. They are grateful for the opportunity to work, they work hard, and they have a sense of loyalty to their employers.

Not expecting a child to be responsible around the home also sets the stage for homework battles. The something-for-nothing child isn't likely to be any more active a participant in his education than he is in his family. His teachers will report that he won't work unless they stand over him, rarely participates in group discussions, and seems to not care whether he makes good or bad grades. Is that any surprise? A child's attitude toward responsibilities at school is simply an extension of what is or is not expected of him at home.

The something-for-nothing child will come home with work that should have been done in class, and he will work as hard at home to avoid doing the work as he did at school. Maybe harder, for home is where the something-for-nothing lesson was learned in the first place and where that same behavior has worked in the past.

Every evening, the child's parents will sit with him at the kitchen table and prod him along until his homework is finally done. They will end up doing too much for him, and once again he will get something for nothing.

And the beat goes on.

Home Reform, Part 3: Teaching Proper Manners

"Manners maketh man." So said William of Wykeham, Bishop of Winchester and Chancellor of England in the fourteenth century. "Manners maketh man" became the motto of Winchester College and New College, Oxford.

Manners were important in Wykeham's day, and they are still important today. Proper manners are not mere personal vanities; they are demonstrations of respect for others. One might not think that teaching children proper manners has anything to do with success in school, but if you talk with teachers as much as I do, you would discover that the children with the best manners are also the children who perform best in class. They listen attentively when the teacher is talking, don't interrupt, wait their turn to speak, offer to help other children, say "please" and "thank you," and rarely, if ever, misbehave. Their good manners are no accident; they learned them at home from parents who assigned high priority to manners and diligently and deliberately taught them.

Teaching proper social etiquette teaches children to "get outside of themselves" and pay attention to others—to anticipate and respond to their needs. Someone is approaching a door; you open it. Someone drops something; you pick it up for them. Someone needs to carry something; you offer to carry it for them. Manners are a form of "other-esteem." Bad manners attract undue attention; good manners do not. Bad manners make people feel uncomfortable; good manners cause other people to feel comfortable, welcome, noticed. Bad manners are self-centered; good manners are other-centered. Good manners are a quiet way of telling people that you care about them. Good manners teach a person to listen, pay attention, and always put one's best foot forward. That explains why so many teachers have told me that children with good manners are their best students.

Teaching manners should be high on one's list of parenting priorities, and the teaching should begin early. Beginning at age three, teach one manner—a social courtesy—every month to your child. Begin with "please" and "thank you." Go from there to not interrupting conversations, proper table manners, and proper manners toward guests, including the child's friends. As the child gets older, introduce opening doors and offering to carry things for people. By the time your child enters school, he'll be well on his way to high achievement.

The importance of proper social decorum was underscored by a 2013 *Time* magazine article that attributed the high youth unemployment rate to bad manners. "Specifically, companies say candidates are lacking in motivation, interpersonal skills, appearance, punctuality and flexibility," *Time* noted. In other words, companies aren't hiring young people because they lack computer or other technical skills; they're not hiring them because they're ill mannered. Many young people don't care about their appearance or presentation and don't seem to care what other people think of them. By the way, that sort of arrogant interpersonal indifference is a symptom of high self-esteem, and according to researchers such as Roy Baumeister at Florida State University, today's youth possess it in abundance.

The *Time* article reminded me of an encounter my wife had with a young person in 2013. Willie was trying to maneuver her way into a parking space in the worst parking lot in Charlotte, North Carolina. It services a highly popular food store, and everyone agrees that both the lanes and spaces are too narrow. I call it a "coach class" parking lot because it's obvious that the planners were trying—as do airlines with coach class passengers—to cram as many cars into the space as possible, with no consideration of customer comfort. Anyway, Willie nosed in, then backed up to try and better align the car with the lines. Bing! She bumped into a car behind her. She put her car in park, got out, and went back to survey the damage.

She encountered a sullen, angry young woman who was staring at a small ding in the fender of her late-model foreign sedan. Before Willie could say anything, the woman shouted. "I don't believe this!" Then, still without looking at Willie, she shouted, "You dented my car!"

"Are you hurt?" Willie asked. The woman still wouldn't look at her and now wouldn't talk. Willie repeated the question.

"No! But look at my car!"

"I'm terribly sorry," Willie said and then excused herself to get her insurance card. When she returned, card in hand, she told the woman that the ding—which didn't even crack the paint—could be worked out at a body shop with little effort or time (Willie's had some experience in these matters herself), but that if the woman preferred, Willie would call the police. The woman said nothing, now alternating between looking at the ding and then staring dramatically into the sky, so Willie just wrote her contact and insurance information on a card and handed it to the woman, who took it without a word.

As Willie walked back to her car, a thought occurred to her. She turned around and walked back over to the woman.

"You know," she said, "Just in case you care, when someone offers you a sincere apology, you really should acknowledge it."

"Whatever."

That's a good example of why employers are complaining they can't find suitable young people to fill available jobs.

Don't allow your kids to treat other people with anything less than respect. That includes dressing appropriately for an occasion, good personal hygiene, looking people in the eye when in conversation, and good manners. Teach your kids the value—to themselves and others—of not only putting one's best foot forward at all times but also of helping other people feel comfortable and showing that you care.

I've asked lots of teachers to tell me what advice they have for parents who want their children to do their best in school. The most common answer is, "Discipline properly at home so that the child comes to school already well-behaved." The second most common answer is, "Teach good manners." The third is, "Back your child's teacher when she reports a discipline problem, and when that happens, discipline the child again at home." The fourth is, "Read to your child a lot during his preschool years."

Not one teacher has ever given me the following answer: "Make sure your child is already reading and knows his or her basic math facts before he comes to kindergarten." But even though the people on education's front line don't seem to think that's very important, most parents think that's the single most valuable thing they can do to promote their children's school success. As a result, they spend money on so-called jump start reading and math programs and flash cards and tutors and expensive preschools that feed expensive private schools and so on and so forth. And they send children who can already read, write, and do basic math to kindergarten.

Part of what's involved in all this is fear. Specifically, the parents are afraid that if their child isn't up to par academically when he enters school, if he's already behind the other kids in his kindergarten class, he'll be behind the academic curve forever, will never get into a good college, and will never reach his full potential as an adult. That's what I call apocalyptic thinking. Unfortunately, it drives a lot of parenting behavior.

Here's what the research consistently says: By the end of the third grade, these artificially induced academic advantages have disappeared. By the end of the third grade, all else being equal, two children of equal ability as measured by IQ tests will be performing at the same level in school even though one of them came to kindergarten already reading and the other, when he came to kindergarten, was "illiterate." In short, a child has just so much potential. That's what IQ tests measure: intellectual (problem-solving) potential. Whether he rises to his potential is not a matter of how much academic knowledge was stuffed into his head during his preschool years. It's a matter of whether he came to school having already learned to pay attention to adults, do what adults tell him to do, and do his best.

This assertion is confirmed historically. In the 1950s, for example, America's classrooms were bursting at the seams with children, the so-called baby boomers. In the early to mid-1950s, the typical elementary school (grades one through eight) class consisted of around thirty-five children taught by one teacher. That's an average, mind you. My first, second, and third grade classes consisted, respectively, of fifty, thirty-seven, and forty-three kids. I've met women who taught elementary classes as large as ninety-five children! No kidding—by themselves! Most baby boomers, me included, came to first grade not knowing their ABCs. Back then, parents prepared their children for school by teaching good manners, insisting on respect and obedience, assigning chores, and insisting that chores be done on time and properly. Teachers taught children to read, write, and do math.

Here's what you may find amazing: At the end of first grade, kids in the 1950s were reading and doing math at a higher level than today's kids. In fact, the baby boomers outperformed today's children at every grade level. We weren't smarter. By all indications, IQ has been steadily rising since the 1950s. Today's kids are smarter, in pure terms, than we were. The explanation for this conundrum is that we came to school having already learned to pay attention to adult authority figures, do what adult authority figures told us to do, and do our best at whatever tasks they assigned us.

William of Wykeham said manners maketh man. I say good manners make the best students.

Home Reform, Part 4: Obedience

Question: Who is happier, an obedient child or a disobedient child? Right, the obedient child! That is common sense, and that is also what parenting research done by people such as psychologists Diana Baumrind and Robert Larzelere (the USA's two leading parenting outcome researchers) has confirmed.

I begin with that question and answer in order to emphasize, from the outset, that obedience is in the best interest of children. Obedience on the part of children certainly makes life easier for their parents, but in the final analysis, the primary beneficiary is the obedient child. According to the best research (Baumrind and Larzelere again), obedient children are happier, do better in school, and are more socially successful. So, adding to what I said earlier in this chapter, the top four predictors of success in school are parents who (1) are married, (2) love each other, (3) teach proper manners, and (4) expect and insist on obedience.

Once upon a time not so long ago, children respected and obeyed adults who occupied positions of legitimate authority (i.e., responsible adults). The exception was rare. Today, the child who respects, defers to, and readily obeys adult authority figures is the exception. Since the 1960s, parents have become increasingly confused about how to discipline children. Much of this confusion has been manufactured by experts who marketed to an unsuspecting public such absurd and destructive notions as the "democratic family" and the "child-centered family" and told parents to do silly things like "get down to your child's level when you talk to him." These experts took the realities of parenthood and replaced them with rhetoric. They took the common sense of raising a child and replaced it with nonsense. In the process, they undermined the confidence of nearly an entire generation of parents, who began to feel as if they had no authority other than that which their children would accept, which was little, if any.

So instead of expecting obedience, which the experts told them they had no right to do, parents began *wishing* for it. Such wishful thinking takes the form of pleading, bargaining, bribing, cajoling, reasoning, explaining, encouraging, promising, threatening, haranguing, and, most of all, arguing with children.

Children don't grant adult wishes. They conform to adult expectations that are communicated clearly, calmly, and unequivocally—in no uncertain terms. Obviously, many parents don't understand that. When their wishes don't come true, these wishful parents become frustrated and complain about their children's behavior. Sometimes they complain to the children themselves, who are not impressed, if the truth were known. Or these parents pound their fists on furniture, become red in the face, and threaten terrible, unthinkable horrors if their children do not immediately obey (e.g., "THAT'S IT! I'VE HAD IT! YOU'RE NOT GETTING ANY CHRISTMAS PRESENTS THIS YEAR!"). This results in temporary obedience, maybe, and further loss of true respect (and no lack of Christmas presents).

"Respect your child," said the experts. "Remember that respect is a two-way street. Your child will respect you only if you show respect for your child." This was part of the rhetoric of the democratic family, a family in which everyone lives in harmony because no one is in control. *Everyone* runs the show. Children are regarded and treated as equal to adults and are therefore consulted about all decisions that might affect their little lives. And everyone lives happily ever after. That's the myth. It's an example of the generally bad advice parenting professionals—psychologists, marriage and family therapists, pediatricians, child development specialists—have given parents since the 1960s. (Bad advice from parenting experts is the subject of my book *Parent-Babble*.)

Here's the truth: Children need parents who are constant in their demonstrations of competence and self-confidence. Children need parents who act as if they are powerful enough to protect and provide for them under any and all circumstances. Self-confident parents ensure a child's sense of security, which in turn frees the child to begin exploring the limits of his or her own potential for competence.

Children need parents who know where they stand and stand firm. If parents stand in one place one minute and in another the next and yet another the next, it becomes impossible for their children to become convinced of their ability to protect and provide for them. These parents are unreliable, and unreliable parents make for insecure children. Their insecurity drives what is called testing behavior, which is nothing more than an anxiety-ridden search for where their parents stand.

The child who constantly tests is really asking, "Please stop moving around, because every time you change positions, every time you are inconsistent, every time you say one thing and do another, every time I am able to wear you down by whining and pleading, every time you give in to one of my tantrums, I am forced to test that much more."

Parents who are inconsistent engage their children in a perpetual game of hide-and-seek, and the fact that their children have no choice but to play consumes enormous amounts of their developmental energies—energies that would otherwise be available for creative pursuits, for self-expansion, for activities that bring success. Testing never brings success. Therefore, it is not possible to test and feel good about yourself at the same time.

I agree that parents should show respect for children. I also agree that respect in the parent–child relationship is a two-way street. But the traffic that moves from parent toward child is and must be vastly different in quality from the traffic that moves from child toward parent. You see, children show respect for parents by obeying them. And parents show respect for children by expecting them to obey.

In short, children need parents who act like Superior Beings. Most parenting experts would cringe at that idea. But as you may have already gathered, I am not most parenting experts. I believe experts have created more problems than they have solved, or even know how to solve, for America's parents. I believe parents will get better advice, generally, from a grandparent than from a parenting expert. I have seven grandchildren. That's the primary reason why you can trust my advice. The capital letters after my name have nothing to do with my credibility.

Again, parents should act like Superior Beings. I am superior to the person I was when I was five, fifteen, or even fifty. You are superior to the person you were when you were a child; therefore, you are superior to your child. Act like it. For one thing, stop stooping down to your child's level when you talk to him. Peers are at the same level. You are not your child's peer. You are a Superior Being. Give instructions and communicate decisions from a superior position. Stand upright. Cause your child to look up to you. Say what you mean and mean what you say. Tell it like it is. Communicate decisions and instructions using the fewest words possible, as in these examples:

- "No."
- "I want these toys picked up and put away now."
- "Sit down, right there, right now."
- "You don't get to order for yourself off the menu until I'm no longer paying for your meal."
- "I have to tell you that I really don't care what you want or why you want it. You're not getting what you want, period."
- "You can feel any way you want about my decision; you simply cannot *do* anything you want."
- "Yes, if I were your age, I would think I was being mean. That's fine. Doesn't change a thing, especially the fact that I love you."

And stop explaining yourself. The problem with explanations is that they sound persuasive. They do not sound authoritative. Superior Beings do not have to justify their decisions to the people beneath them. Your children are beneath you. They were created equal, but that doesn't mean they are your equals. When Thomas Jefferson wrote "all Men are created equal" in the opening to the Declaration of Independence, he meant we are all equal in the sight of God. By no means did he mean that children were equal to adults. To the founders, children were inferior to adults, which is why the founders did not intend for the rights enumerated in the Constitution to be extended to children. Children were inferior to adults in the late 1700s, as they were before that time, and they are still inferior to adults. Your children are inferior to you. Therefore, you do not have to ever justify your decisions to your children. Because explanations are not authoritative, they are not the stuff of effective leadership; they invite push-back, which quickly turns into argument, which quickly deteriorates into anger on the part of one or both parties.

In graduate school, I was immersed in psychobabble. It took me a good while to learn that my graduate school experience was more of a hindrance to me—in both my personal and professional lives—than a help. I began questioning everything I'd learned in school and found myself discarding the new stuff and embracing the old stuff, one piece at a time. One of the pieces of old stuff I embraced is the Universal, All-Purpose, Truthful Explanation for All Parent Decisions: "Because I said so." Not screamed, but simply and calmly stated. The truth contained therein is that most of your parenting decisions are arbitrary. Why does your child have to keep his room clean? The arbitrariness of your expectation is proven by the fact that his friends' parents don't make them keep their rooms clean. So, the *only* reason your child has to keep his room clean is because you want it that way. Period.

So from now on, when your child demands to know the why or why not of a decision you make, you have my permission—the permission of one of America's leading parenting experts (but more importantly, a grandfather)—to say, "Because I said so." And then, turn around and walk away.

I'm not advocating a repressive, totalitarian form of parent government. I'm advocating for effective parent leadership. Everyone needs effective leadership in their lives. Everyone, whether they know it or not, benefits from having people to look up to. Such is the case with children. Give your children someone to look up to. Act like a Superior Being.

Home Reform, Part 5: Resourcefulness Training

According to my dictionary, a resourceful person is one who uses his or her "fullest capacity for finding, adapting, or inventing means of solving problems." School is a problem-solving environment. It stands to reason that the more resourceful a child is, the better student he or she will also be.

The resourceful student will be far less likely to cash in his chips when confronted with a difficult problem than one who is not so equally endowed. To a resourceful child, a difficult problem presents simply another opportunity to explore, experiment, adapt, or invent, all of which bring pleasure in and of themselves. The resourceful child is able to think more flexibly, more creatively. His ability to examine any given situation from a variety of perspectives means he is more adept at trial-and-error, the essence of "if at first you don't succeed, try, try again."

Resourceful people enjoy being challenged. They love to clear hurdles and are always looking for higher ones. If they fall short of their goals, they become that much more determined. Resourceful people regard dejection and despair as a waste of time. In short, resourceful people are the winners of the world.

Every child, regardless of IQ, has a potential for being greatly resourceful. Developing that potential begins with the child learning to entertain himself, which will develop naturally as long as he does not become dependent on parents, toys, or electronics for entertainment. And make sure you give your child plenty of Vitamin "N" (No!). Let's take these ideas one at a time.

Don't Become Your Child's Playmate

I'm not saying you should never, ever engage in play with your child. I'm saying that should not be a daily thing, something your child expects of you, something he depends on. Occasional parent–child play is fine. But there is a line between being occasionally playful with your child and being your child's playmate. Make sure you stay on the "occasional" side of the line. The less you entertain, the more he has to figure out how to entertain himself. And remember, that's how resourcefulness begins to develop.

Buy Your Child Very Few Toys

A resourceful person is able to do a lot with a little. The same rule applies to children. It follows that the fewer toys a child has, the better able he or she will be to develop the potential for resourcefulness. This is historically validated. In the 1950s and before, the typical child had few toys. In 1952, when I was five years old, I had five toys: a set of Lincoln Logs, a set of Tinker Toys, an electric train, a small set of lead cavalry and foot soldiers, and a cap pistol. I don't remember being bored, ever. Today's typical child, by age five, has received more than three hundred toys. And yet he complains frequently of being bored. A child's complaint of boredom is a sign that he isn't getting in touch with his potential for resourcefulness. Just as parents being playmates inhibits resourcefulness, so do too many toys. Ironically, the more toys a child has, the less resourceful the child will be. Just as children quickly become dependent on parents who are playmates, children become quickly dependent on getting new toys. You can easily tell if you have a toy-dependent child: He plays with a new toy for a few days or a week, stops playing with it, and begins again to complain of being bored. If that child is living with you, it's time to give the toys he's not playing with to a charity and stop buying new toys.

Don't Let Your Child Become Dependent for Entertainment on Television, Video Games, or Computers

Nearly every human being is born already programmed for intelligence, creativity, and an incredible variety of other skills. During the formative years, these skills are activated by exposing the child to environments and experiences that push the right genetic buttons. Releasing the richness of each child's developmental birthright simply requires that he have sufficient opportunity for exploration, discovery, and imaginative play. Environments and experiences that stimulate and exercise these emerging skills are therefore compatible with a growing child's developmental needs, but environments that fail to offer these important opportunities are incompatible.

Consider how electronic devices fit into this relationship between environment and development. The average American child watches more than five thousand hours of television during his preschool years, much more time than is spent in any other single activity. In effect, television has become a primary environment for America's preschool children and must therefore be affecting their development greatly.

The question then becomes, "What competency skills are being exercised as a child watches television?"

The answer: None.

Watching television doesn't engage or involve visual tracking, active problem solving, fine or gross motor skills, social skills, communication, inquiry, exploration, initiative, motivation, imagination, creativity, or achievement. Furthermore, because of the incessant flicker of a television screen, watching television doesn't help a child develop a long attention span. Incidentally, these are the skills that a child must bring to school in order to become a successful reader.

The developmental skills that make up and support the act of reading are acquired in the preschool years during the most natural childhood activity, play. Television watching is not a natural or playful activity. In fact, it is not an activity at all but a *passivity*. It is a deprivational experience that masquerades as fun.

Evidence that television has taken its toll on the competency and literacy of America's children can be found in the fact that since 1965, when television became a fixture in nearly every American home, academic achievement at all grade levels has declined and learning disabilities have become epidemic. It is not at all coincidental that a list of learning disability symptoms closely parallels the aforementioned list of deficiencies inherent in watching television.

Electronic devices with screens are the dominant factor in the life of today's typical child. My generation watched television. My children's generation watched television and played rudimentary video games such as Pong and Mario Brothers. Today's kids are growing up with television, highly sophisticated and often violent video games, personal computers, tablets, and cell phones. Electronics have radically changed the nature of childhood. Fifty years ago, children played outdoors. Today, if one drives through a residential neighborhood, even on a weekend or in the summer, it is rare to see a group of kids playing outside. For today's kids, outdoor play consists primarily of adult-organized, adult-directed sports. In my estimation, that's not play. It's performance. Play is spontaneous, child-organized and child-directed (if the word *direction* even applies), creative, imaginative, and open-ended. When children are truly playing, rules are always somewhat loose.

For the last twenty-five years, researchers have been looking into the issue of how electronic devices are affecting children. Their findings:

- Electronic devices, especially video games, are literally addictive. They are the childhood equivalent of adult addictions to gambling, pornography, and shopping.
- Television and video games shorten your attention span.
- Computers interfere with reasoning skills.
- As screen time increases, academic performance decreases.
- Electronic devices have a negative impact on brain development.
- Electronic devices have a negative impact on social aptitude, including communication skills and interpersonal empathy.
- Electronic device use is associated with poor self-control.

Parents often seek my help concerning children who exhibit major behavior problems: anger issues, poor social skills, disrespect, disobedience, belligerence, lack of motivation, poor school performance, antagonism toward siblings, teasing, and sometimes outright cruelty toward family pets. Many of these parents portray children—usually boys—who spend nearly all their time in their rooms behind locked doors, refusing to even participate in family meals. When describing these kids, parents use words such as *sullen, negative, easily irritated, moody, petulant,* and *sneaky.* Without realizing it, these parents are describing symptoms of clinical depression and sociopathy.

When I ask, "What does your son do in his room?" they answer, with rare exception, "He watches television and plays video games." The video games in question are violent, dark, and often demonic. Some of these games even involve murder, violence toward women, and overt sexuality.

Bombarding a child's developing brain with electronic images is bad enough. Bombarding it with images that are violent, perverse, immoral, and demonic is beyond bad. Words like *horrific, appalling,* and *toxic* come to mind. The epidemic numbers of preadolescent and adolescent males addicted to video games is a chilling signal for America's future.

The amazing thing is that when I point out to these parents that their children are addicted to video games and tell them what researchers have found about the impact of screen-based electronics on social skills, self-control, emotional development, academic performance, and so on, *some of these parents will not remove the video game consoles and other devices from their kids' rooms and get rid of them.* The excuse most often given is that the child in question lives for his video games, that playing online games is the only social life he has, that it's the only thing that seems to bring him any pleasure, and that they're afraid of what he might do if he came home from school to find that his video game, computer, and television were gone. And they don't come back for another appointment.

But then there are those parents who have the courage to cold turkey their kids off these sources of electronic poison. Their stories are inspiring. They tell of kids who, when electronics are removed completely from their lives, slowly begin acting like normal human beings. One set of parents told me that when their fifteen-year-old son came home from school to find that the video game console, computer, and television had been removed from his room (and disposed of in a landfill), he went into a rage and virtually destroyed his room. For two weeks, if he wasn't at school, he was in his room, brooding. Occasionally, he would begin screaming, throwing things, and kicking holes in his wall. The parents held on, as terrified as they were. What courage! After two weeks of withdrawal, the youngster began coming out of his room for meals. Two weeks later, he voluntarily cleaned his room for the first time in years. Within several more weeks, he was calling other kids and making plans to do things with them (the parents would not let him go to a friend's home if there was a video game console in his room). The boy's grades began improving. Two months passed with things getting slowly but steadily better; then one day, the young fellow sat down with his parents and said, "I need to thank you for taking my video games away. I was an addict. I feel a whole lot better about myself and everything else now."

I became aware that one of my grandchildren was becoming addicted to video games. When I spent time with him, it was all he wanted to talk about. My attempt to talk with him about anything else was met with monosyllables like "yeah" and incoherent grunts. His eye contact was poor. I shared my concern with his parents. They had a hard time accepting that my concerns were valid, but they listened. A year later, during a visit, this same grandchild was conversational, his affect was greatly improved, and when I asked what was going on in his life, he did not even mention video games. Privately, I mentioned how pleased I was to his parents.

They said, "You were right. He was addicted to video games. They're gone."

Several years later this same grandchild, now in junior high school, told my wife and me that if he was still playing video games he'd be a zombie. We all had a good laugh.

What's not funny at all is that for every kid who might have become a video game zombie if not for parental courage, there are dozens of kids whose childhoods have been irreparably damaged by these nefarious devices. These kids will never be the human beings they could have become.

I'd shout, "DON'T LET YOUR KIDS HAVE VIDEO GAMES, TELEVISIONS, OR THE INTERNET IN THEIR ROOMS!" from the rooftops if I could be certain the guys in white jackets wouldn't come, truss me up in a stainless steel straitjacket, and take me away in a portable rubber room. Instead, I talk about it at every possible opportunity because I believe, more than I believe just about anything else, that every child has an inalienable right to become as complete and competent a human being as he or she was meant to become.

Turn off the electronics and turn on your child!

Administer Liberal Doses of Vitamin "N"

Say "No" to his requests more often than you say "Yes." "No" is the most character-building two-letter word in the English language. Children who hear it sufficiently often learn to tolerate frustration. This tolerance enables them to persevere in the face of obstacles and adversity, and perseverance—need I remind you?—is the essential ingredient in any success story. Whether the pursuit is vocational, avocational, social, or spiritual, perseverance makes the difference between those who consistently reach their goals and those who don't. It may sound strange to say, but if you want to help your child develop a successful attitude toward the challenges of life, you must not be afraid to frustrate him. In order to equip a child with the skills he will need to pursue happiness on his own, the skills he will need to achieve success in life, parents must be courageous enough to make that child occasionally and temporarily unhappy. In order to help a child learn to stand on his own two feet, parents must not prop him up with one material thing after another. It's important that parents know the difference between what children truly need and what they simply want. It then becomes important that parents give children all that they truly need along with a conservative amount of what they simply want. This prudent conservatism forces a child to figure out certain things for himself. In effect, his parents are saying, "We won't figure everything out for you." Under the circumstances, he has no choice but to become more ingenious, more adaptable, more inventive, creative, and self-reliant. That is, more resourceful.

Final Word

I once heard an educator say that parents should visit their child's classroom on a regular basis. He said they should establish a presence in what he called "their child's primary learning environment."

In the first place, a child's primary learning environment is the home, not the school. In the second, regardless of how often they visit and even if they never visit at all, parents *do* establish a presence in their child's classroom. Every day a child goes to school, he takes his parents with him in the form of their discipline, their expectations, and their values. And the child's performance in school reflects that presence—the degree to which his parents have succeeded in preparing him for the responsibilities his teachers will expect of him.

I have a slightly different take on the issue of parental involvement: The best way to get involved, the best way to support the efforts of your children's teachers, is to put first things first. At home, concentrate on building strong foundations for learning and excellence by teaching the three *R*s of Respect, Responsibility, and Resourcefulness. As I have said, teachers cannot do what parents are supposed to do. They can only *capitalize* on what parents have already accomplished and are continuing to reinforce.

A child's education is a two-handed process. On the one hand are responsibilities that belong to the schools. On the other hand are responsibilities that belong to the child's parents. Only if those hands are joined will the child's education be truly complete.

2

The Hassle

The story behind this book has been told to me by hundreds of parents over the years. The specifics vary from one teller to another, but it generally goes something like this:

"Billy is in the third grade, and we're having a problem getting him to do his work. His teacher has to almost stand over him to get him to do anything at all during the day; otherwise, he'll just sit and piddle or talk to the children around him. As a result, he's supposed to bring home not only whatever homework has been assigned but also the classwork he's failed to finish. In the past, however, he's lied to us about whether or not he has homework and how much, so before he leaves school, he has to write his assignments down in an assignment notebook and take the list to his teacher, who checks it for accuracy and initials it.

"When he gets home, the first thing I [the speaker is always, without exception, the child's mother] do is go over the assignments with him, making sure he knows what he's supposed to do and that he has the necessary books and materials. But sometimes he forgets—at least he *says* he forgets—to write his assignments in the notebook, and I guess the teacher gets caught up in other things and doesn't ask to check it, in which case I either have to rely on his word or call another parent. I've even called the teacher at home, and there have been more than a few times when I've driven back up to the school to get books or other things he's forgotten.

"So [heavy sigh], once we get everything together, I sit him down at the kitchen table where I can supervise and provide whatever help he needs, and we get started. Except he does the same thing with me he does in class: He just sits and piddles unless I'm right there. So I end up sitting with him, explaining the work step-by-step, and sometimes—I have to admit—dictating things to him so all he has to do is write down what I'm saying. I know that means I'm sort of doing his work for him, but sometimes I just can't help it; I get so frustrated waiting for him to put pencil to paper.

"I mean, he sometimes acts like he doesn't have a brain. We go over a problem on Monday, and I'm sure he knows how to do it, but he draws a blank on Tuesday. So we go over it again, but then it's the same old story on Wednesday. I know he's smart, his teacher knows he's smart, and there isn't anything he *wants* to do that he can't do, but schoolwork just seems to anesthetize his circuits or something. I don't know what it is. All I know is it's driving me slowly nuts. If I manage to survive this with my sanity intact, it'll be a miracle.

"So anyway, from the time Billy gets home until supper—in between trying to cook, answer the phone, and take care of the other kids—I'm helping him with homework. I guess you could say my life isn't my own. Billy's dad gets home around six, at which point we clear the table of books and other homework stuff and set the table for supper. After we finish eating, we clear the table and back come the books.

"You can generally find me helping Billy with his homework until eight o'clock. But wait! Billy has baseball practice after supper on Tuesdays and Thursdays and a piano lesson after school on Wednesday. On those days, we might be up with homework until nine or ten. No joke!

"In the morning, before he leaves for school, I make sure Billy's book bag is packed properly. I learned that lesson after having to drive his homework to school a couple of times because he left it at home.

"I just don't understand it. The mothers of other children in his class tell me it takes their kids thirty, maybe forty-five minutes a night to do their homework. It takes us three or four hours. Granted, Billy's got to finish work he should have finished in class, but even that shouldn't keep us at the kitchen table more than an hour and thirty minutes, at most.

"By the time we're done, I'm a wreck. Sometimes I lose my patience and start screaming at Billy, which makes him cry, which makes me feel like a total failure. Then my husband comes in and gets mad at Billy for getting me upset, and I defend him, saying it isn't his fault, and it's downhill from there.

"How do I explain all this to myself? Sometimes I think Billy must have some problem, maybe some learning problem or something, but he does well on the standardized tests they give at the end of the year. Then I think maybe he has low self-esteem and that this is just his way of getting me to pay attention to him. Maybe I haven't paid enough attention to him since the other kids came along. Maybe he feels neglected or something, I don't know. My best friend says Billy's manipulating me, but I don't see how that could be. After all, he's not enjoying our homework sessions any more than I am, so if he's manipulating me, he's sort of cutting off his nose to spite his face, don't you think?"

Whew!

The Names of the Games

Although the specific details may differ from one child to the next, there are certain key elements in this scenario that are present nearly every time the story is told.

First, there's "The Great Homework Hunt," also known as "Homework Hide-and-Seek." This is where Mom goes through great contortions trying to figure out just exactly what work Billy (or Susie) is supposed to do that evening. Mom riffles through Billy's book bag in search of clues, she combs his notebooks for evidence, calls other parents, calls the teacher, consults Billy's astrological chart or some ancient mystical document, and all the while, Billy just sits there. Doing nothing. That's his role—or one aspect of it anyway—in this daily drama: Do nothing.

Next, we have a prime example of "Parenting by Helicopter." Note that Mom has Billy do his homework at the kitchen or dining room table so that she can supervise, meaning she hovers over him, prodding and bribing and cajoling and directing and doing things for Billy that he's perfectly capable of doing for himself, all the while becoming more and more flustered. That's Mom's role: Do everything for Do Nothing.

Meanwhile, Billy plays "Duh, I'm Dumb." In his mother's words, he acts "like he doesn't have a brain." He forgets things that have been drilled into his head for days. He can't think of anything to write for an instruction as simple as "Write a sentence containing the words *I, sat,* and *table.*" His writing hand moves only slightly quicker than a fly in molasses. He adds when he should subtract, circles when he should underline, and generally acts like he's taken a horse tranquilizer.

This all culminates in the "Homework Marathon," in which thirty minutes of homework takes three hours. As I write, the formula for finding the actual length of the marathon is being worked on by the same team of astrophysicists who finally answered the question, "Who put the bop in the bop shoo bop shoo bop?" Finally, Billy and his parents play "We're a Bunch of Bananas." After beating her head against the same old brick wall for hours, Mom has a massive cerebral meltdown, which causes Billy to begin wailing at the top of his lungs, which makes Dad furious, which causes Mom to get between Dad and Billy, which makes Dad even more furious, which ruins everybody's evening, if it wasn't already ruined, and then everyone goes to bed and has horrible nightmares in which they're being chased by huge erasers, bent on rubbing them out.

In the junior high and high school versions of this melodrama, Billy's parents don't know anything is wrong until midterm reports come in. Sometimes, somehow, Billy intercepts e-mails from the school (he's actually a technological genius), and his parents, thinking no news is good news, ask no questions. If his parents do manage to get their hands on the midterm reports, Billy invents all sorts of excuses to explain his poor grades.

He says things like, "I just made an A on a test that wasn't included in the report, so, like, chill out, 'cause my report card grade should be at least a B." Then he gives his parents his "you are really pitiful" look.

Or, "Everybody got bad midterm grades because of this one really hard test that nobody passed, but the teacher said he might not even count that test for the final grade, so this is really no big deal, ya know?" I told you, Billy's a genius.

Several weeks later, report cards come out and his grades aren't any better, and Billy promises he'll do better, except maybe in algebra because, he explains, "My teacher doesn't like me." When his parents threaten to restrict him, he says, "If you restrict me, you'll take away the only reasons I have for doing good work in school." For some reason, this actually makes sense to Billy's parents.

Eventually, they talk to the guidance counselor, who promises to meet with Billy on a regular basis to make sure he's keeping up with his work. She also says she'll check in every Friday with Billy's teachers to see how he's doing and make sure he gets whatever extra help he needs. Billy forgets his first meeting with the counselor. She chases him down and schedules another, which he can't make because something really important came up at the last minute and, uh, well, you know the rest.

A Question of Accountability

The fundamental question, over which there appears to be much confusion, is "Whose homework is it anyway?"

It's Billy's, right? Right, but no one's acting like it is. Billy's parents, teachers, and (in the junior high/high school version) guidance counselor have—without realizing what they're doing, and certainly with the very purest of intentions—appropriated responsibility for Billy's school performance. Mind you, none of these folks would disagree that the responsibility belongs to Billy. Nonetheless, their behavior belies that simple fact. These very well-intentioned adults have taken Billy's problem—his failure to do his schoolwork—away from him and made it their own, emotionally and otherwise.

Proof that the emotional responsibility for the problem no longer rests with Billy: When Billy fails to do his schoolwork, who gets upset? Billy's parents and, to a lesser extent, Billy's teacher or teachers, that's who! Billy doesn't get upset at all. That's proof that the adults in Billy's life have shouldered the emotional consequences of Billy's problem.

Proof that the practical, concrete responsibility for the problem no longer rests with Billy: When Billy fails to do his schoolwork, who does something about it? Again, Billy's parents, teachers, and guidance counselor. They monitor, supervise, hover, confer, and ask lots of neurotic questions like, "Is your homework done?" Meanwhile, Billy does nothing. Well, that's not exactly true. He does a lot of things, but nothing that he does results in schoolwork getting done. He dodges, deceives, dinks around, acts dumb, and dishes up a lot of hokum whenever he's confronted with the facts.

As things stand, Billy has absolutely no reason to change his ways. He's off the hook. And as long as adults continue to do for Billy what he ought to do (and is certainly capable of doing) for himself, as long as they continue feeling for Billy what he ought to be feeling about himself (i.e., mad, frustrated, guilty), he has complete permission to continue being irresponsible.

Every night, Monday through Thursday, homework occupies center stage in Billy's family. It becomes the primary focus of family activity. It attracts more energy and attention than any other issue. Everything stops, or is left to just stumble along, until Billy finishes his homework. His parents' marriage stops, domestic responsibilities are done catch-as-catch-can, siblings are left to fend for themselves, the family dog goes off and curls up in a corner. And whom do we find sitting complacently at the center of the homework hurricane? Billy. He's the central character in this nightly soap opera. Moreover, he's both the victim and the villain, depending on whether his mother is feeling guilty or angry. Most confusing!

Homework doesn't belong at center stage in a family. Homework doesn't *deserve* this much attention. When it's allowed to work its way into the family spotlight, there will be nothing but trouble. People will lose track of whose homework it is, and as in the case of Billy's mother, their typical attempts to solve the homework problem will only make it worse.

The Parent Trap

Some people—even some professionals—might say that Billy is using homework to manipulate and get attention from his parents. But the fact that a certain behavior results in the child being the center of adult attention doesn't mean the child is *seeking* that adult attention. Besides, young children are generally incapable of thinking in sophisticated and insightful terms about themselves and the impact their behavior is having on others. They don't sit around conspiring against their parents, devising clever ways of pulling the proverbial rug out from under them.

Problems of this sort usually have their roots early in the child's development. In most instances, they stem from precedents set before the child was four years old. The manner in which parents handle certain issues when they first come up in the parent–child relationship not only sets the tone for how the same and similar issues will be handled in the future but also determines how ongoing they will be. In particular, if parents set dysfunctional precedents concerning responsibility and autonomy—the two issues most germane to the subject of homework—then these issues will keep coming up in the parent–child relationship. And each time the issue comes up, it's likely to wear a new disguise.

For example, when it was time for Billy to learn to use the toilet, his parents hovered anxiously over him, worrying about accidents. Their hovering interfered with Billy's ability to take autonomous responsibility for this important learning process. The more they hovered, the more accidents he had. The more accidents he had, the more anxious his parents became, and the more they hovered.

Unbeknownst to Billy's parents, they were not only their own and Billy's worst enemy, they were also building a trap that would ensnare all of them whenever the issues of responsibility and autonomy arose in the parent–child relationship. As with toilet training, when these issues first came up no one learned to handle them in a functional manner. So when they came up again in a different form, people just fell back into their same old dysfunctional ways.

When it was time for Billy to start picking up after himself around the house and keep his room orderly, he started having accidents. The more accidents he had, the more his parents hovered and nagged, and nothing was accomplished. To this day, he still does not pick up after himself or keep his room straight. Who does? Guess.

When it was time for Billy to begin getting up in the morning and dressing himself on time for school, he started having accidents. He dinked around in the morning, and that aroused his parents' anxiety and caused them to begin hovering, so nothing was accomplished. To this day, he still does not get up by himself and prepare himself properly and on time for school. Who gets him up? Who makes sure he gets to school on time? Guess.

Billy never learned to entertain himself either. Early on, his parents entertained him, and when they weren't doing it, he was entertained with television. His parents felt it was their responsibility to keep him occupied, so in effect, they became his playmates.

He never learned to go to sleep on his own either. When he was an infant, one of his parents sat with him, rocking him until he was asleep. When he became too big to rock, one of them still sat with him, singing to him and stroking his back until he fell asleep. Billy became dependent on this, and at age nine he still needs a parent in his room until he falls asleep.

So when it was time for Billy to accept responsibility for his homework, guess what? Right! He started having accidents and acting helpless, and sure enough, his parents stepped right in. Billy and his parents go 'round and 'round in the same old rut. This is not manipulation. This is not attention-seeking behavior. This is a soap opera, and no one knows quite how they got into the roles they're playing. No one knows exactly what they're doing, no one knows why they're doing it, and no one knows how to stop.

In this case, I put Billy's mother in the central role because I wanted to illustrate a truth about our culture: Mothers are more likely to feel personally responsible for their children's problems than are fathers. The average, middle-class American mom takes pretty much for granted that if her child fails to measure up to one standard or another—whether behavioral, social, or academic—that shortcoming is in some way indicative of a failing or inadequacy on *her* part. Our culture sends some very dysfunctional messages to women, and right up there at the top of the list is, "Once you have children, you're only as worthwhile a human being as your kids are well behaved, do well in school, achieve social success, and so on."

This message is operational even if a woman with children works outside the home. To see the truth in what I'm saying, ask yourself, "What do we call a woman who has children and works outside the home?" The answer is "working mother." Let that sink in a minute. Do you begin to see the implications of that seemingly innocuous phrase? Now, ask yourself, "What do we call a man who has children and works outside the home?" We don't call him a "working father," do we? We call him a "guy with a job"—a plumber, a doctor, a mechanic, or whatever.

The phrase "working mother" implies that by choosing to work outside the home, you must understand and accept that you are depriving your children of something that no one else can provide adequately for them: *your* attention.

As a result, in order to expiate the guilt that comes from deciding to do something for herself (not to mention something that improves her children's standard of living), something independent of her roles as wife and mother, when the working mother gets home from her job, she beats herself into what I call a quality-time frenzy in the name of making up to her children what she thinks she has so selfishly deprived them of for the past eight or nine hours. So to Billy's mother, whether she has an outside job or not, Billy's performance in school is a direct reflection of her own competency as his so-called primary parent.

Because mothers tend to measure their self-worth in terms of their children's behavior and performance, they're also the first to panic when things go wrong; their children's mistakes and problems give rise to the fear that they might be bad mothers. The ensuing panic drives counterproductive behavior of the kind Billy's mother is displaying. And while Mom panics, Dad is all too likely to sit in the den, watching television or reading the newspaper. This is not his problem, or so say the messages we send to dads. He's responsible for maintaining his family's standard of living, not seeing to it that the kids get their homework done.

Don't misunderstand me. I'm definitely, absolutely not suggesting that Dad should be an equally active participant in the panic over Billy's homework. Quite the contrary. I'm suggesting that the whole situation is convoluted and needs a major overhaul. *Everyone's* role in this drama needs to change, and until that happens, everyone will stay in the same rut, night after night after night after night after night.

How to Slice a Banana

Bear with me while I tell another story, this time about a thirty-five-year-old named Myron. Myron likes to play golf on the weekends. He's just your basic weekend golfer, and like many of his breed, he's afflicted with what's known as the banana-ball or slice.

For the uninitiated, a slice is when the ball curves hugely to the right (or left, in the case of a left-handed golfer), and instead of traveling straight toward the target, it lands in tall grass, woods, water, or beyond the out-of-bounds markers. When a golfer develops a slice, it affects every shot he or she hits, except putts.

Myron's solution to the banana-ball is simple: He aims to the left. This increases the likelihood that the ball, after traveling its wayward course, will come down in the general vicinity of his target. In other words, instead of going to a golf professional to discover the cause of the slice and truly *correct* it, Myron simply *compensates* for it by aiming to the left.

The compensation of aiming left doesn't address the problem, but it does conceal, to one degree or another, its consequences. Myron still has a banana-ball, but if he's lucky, it bananas where he wants it to banana, so he's generally satisfied.

The problem is that as long as Myron compensates for his tendency to slice, the worse the slice will get. Over time, you see, the problems that are causing the slice become more and more embedded in Myron's grip, swing, or stance. As those problems become habit, Myron must aim further and further left, compensating for a slice that's getting more and more bananas.

Myron finally sees the light and consults a golf professional about his banana ball. The golf professional takes Myron out to the practice tee and has him aim straight toward the target.

"But," protests Myron, pointing to the right, "I'll hit it over that fence."

"That's all right," answers the pro. "Just bear with me."

Myron swings and hits the ball over the fence.

"See," he says, with noticeable irritation.

"I see," says the pro. "Now, hit another one."

The next ball goes over the fence, too. And the next and the next and the next. Meanwhile, the professional makes a few small adjustments in Myron's grip. Sure enough, the slice becomes slightly less pronounced, but it's still there.

After about thirty minutes, the professional says, "Come back in a week, but if you play a round of golf before the next time I see you, I want you to promise me that you'll always aim straight at the target, no matter how badly you're hitting the ball or how badly you're scoring."

"I promise," says Myron.

The next time Myron plays golf, he follows the pro's advice, loses a dozen balls, shoots the worst score of his life, and has no fun at all. The next time he sees the pro, he's fuming.

"See what your advice has done to my game!" he yells, waving the scorecard in the pro's face.

"Myron," the pro calmly says, "Didn't anyone ever tell you that things will get worse before they get better?"

This very wise golf pro has brought Myron face-to-face with not just one but three facts of life:

- First, you cannot *correct* a problem and *compensate* for it at the same time. Compensation and correction are two mutually exclusive, incompatible strategies. In order to correct a problem that you've been previously compensating for, you must first stop all compensations.

◆ Second, the longer you compensate for a problem, the worse it gets. Compensating only hides the consequences of the problem while allowing it to steadily worsen.

◆ Third (and therefore), when you stop compensating for a problem, when you stop hiding the consequences of it and get down to the business of truly *correcting* it, things will get worse before they get better.

When you stop compensating for a problem, that forces it to shed its disguise and come out of hiding. Now that it's fully visible, it looks really bad, for sure. Worse than ever, because you're no longer concealing its consequences. Ah, but the good news is that now that the problem is out in the open, you can begin to solve it! You can't solve a problem unless it's completely out in the open, now can you? Of course not! So not only do problems get worse before they get better, they absolutely *must* get worse *in order to get better*.

Sometimes, bringing a problem out in the open is all you need to do to solve it. A wise man once said, "The best cure for a problem, any problem, is sunlight."

Back to Billy

Billy's parents are doing the same thing about Billy's failure to do his classwork that Myron was doing about his banana ball. Instead of addressing the root cause of the problem, along with his teacher and guidance counselor (in the junior high school and high school version), they are *compensating* for it. His teacher is checking and initialing Billy's assignment notebook; his mother goes on "The Great

Homework Hunt" and then makes sure Billy has everything he needs to do his work; she orchestrates the "Homework Marathon" and makes sure the homework's in his book bag before he leaves for school in the morning. In the junior high/high school version, the guidance counselor runs around like the proverbial headless chicken because Billy won't cooperate with the help she's extending to him. All these are examples of "aiming left."

And the longer everyone compensates, the more bananas everyone except Billy gets, and the worse the problem becomes because the root cause isn't being addressed.

What's the root cause? To put it in simple terms, Billy's lazy. Call it irresponsibility, if you prefer a bigger word. And the more everyone else hovers and takes on his responsibilities, the more lazy or irresponsible Billy becomes.

Similarly, in order to cure Billy's problem, everyone will have to stop compensating for it. Everyone will have to let it come out in the open and expose it to the curative powers of the sun. That means everyone must stop being responsible for Billy's homework and let Billy be responsible for it on his own. In other words, everyone will have to do pretty much *absolutely nothing*. They're going to have to stop aiming left.

I can hear some readers saying, "Do nothing? You must be kidding!"

That's right, do nothing, at least for a time. Let the problem come out in the open. Stop trying to hide it. Remember the first of our three facts of life? You can't correct a problem and compensate for it at the same time. No one will know just exactly what the problem looks like until it can be seen in its awful entirety. The teacher needs to stop checking Billy's assignment notebook. If he wants to write his assignments down, fine. If not, that's fine too. His mother needs to stop going on the Great Homework Hunt, stop hovering, stop orchestrating the Homework Marathon, stop working up to We're a Bunch of Bananas, and stop making sure his book bag is correctly packed in the morning. In short, stop being such a responsible parent and let Billy come to grips with some responsibility for a change. It's high time, wouldn't you agree?

"But won't that just give Billy permission to be as lazy as he wants?"

Now you're getting it! Remember, the problem has to get worse before it can get better. That's the way it is in golf, that's the way it is in homework, and that's probably the way it is in all of life, wherever and whenever people compensate for problems instead of doing what they must to truly solve them.

At this point, many of you out there in Readerville probably think I'm completely off my rocker. You're shaking your heads, making little noises of confusion and disgust—you may even be a moment or two away from throwing this book in the trash. If you're upset with me, it's only because I'm disturbing the compensations that have become embedded in your thought processes. You see, for every compensation that takes place in a person's behavior, there is a parallel compensation in his or her thinking. As I disturb those compensations, things get worse before they get better. In other words, you get upset. If you'll bear with me, however, things will get better—slowly. Remember, Rome wasn't built in a day, and Myron did eventually learn how to hit the ball straight.

Why Is Homework Important Anyway?

Good question, and before we go any further, it needs an answer. Homework is important for reasons that are obvious and some that are not so obvious. Unfortunately, most people—teachers and parents alike—see no further than the obvious. The immediate aim of assigning homework is to provide children with an opportunity to practice and strengthen academic skills. By devoting adequate time to homework, children stand a better chance of making good grades.

But homework is important for reasons other than good grades. Homework can and should be a character-building experience, a stepping-stone toward emancipation. Managed properly by teachers and parents who appreciate its hidden values, homework can help a child become equipped with certain very essential emotional and behavioral skills, skills he will eventually need to negotiate the often complex demands of adult life. These include the skills of responsibility, autonomy, perseverance, time management, initiative, self-reliance, and resourcefulness.

Let's take a closer look at each of those seven attributes, which I call the Seven Hidden Values of Homework.

Responsibility: The ability to assume ownership of that which rightly belongs to you, to fulfill your obligations, to pick up the ball without hesitation when it bounces into your court, to hold yourself fully accountable for both your mistakes and your successes. Homework is a responsibility that rightfully belongs to the child, not his or her parents. When parents get too involved, they set the process on its head. The lessons get done, but the real lesson isn't learned.

Autonomy: To be self-governing, to stand on your own two feet, the antithesis of dependence. Homework is the first time someone other than a parent assigns tasks to the child on a consistent basis. In that sense, homework breaks new ground. The child is now accountable *outside* the family. The manner in which this golden opportunity is managed will either enhance or obstruct the child's gradual emancipation.

Perseverance: To confront challenge with determination, to strive in spite of difficulties, to complete what you set out to accomplish. If the Little Train That Could had had a Mother Train who, upon seeing her child struggle up the mountain, got behind and pushed, there would have been no point to the story. Likewise, there's no point to a child doing homework if every time the child becomes frustrated, parents absorb that frustration and make it all better. It's a sad fact that many, if not most, of today's parents act as if one of their primary tasks is that of protecting their children from frustration. They seem to believe that standing aside and letting a child grapple with frustration—especially when the grappling could have been prevented—is neglectful, perhaps even abusive. Little do they realize that more often than not, making a child's life easier in the present will only make his adult life more difficult.

Time Management: The ability to organize time in an effective, productive manner, to complete tasks on schedule without compromising quality. In this regard, it is unfortunate that most parents tell children when to start their homework but not when it must be finished. This sets the stage for a nightly homework marathon. Instead of learning to manage time, the child learns to waste it.

Initiative: To be self-motivated and assertive, to be decisive in defining and pursuing personal goals. It boils down to this: Who decides when it's time for the child to begin his homework? Initiative is like a muscle. If it's exercised, it strengthens. On the other hand, if other people are assuming initiative for the child, he will not ever develop the strength to exercise it on his own.

Self-Reliance: To have trust and self-confidence in your abilities. Managed properly, homework empowers, affirms, enlarges, fulfills, actualizes, and enables the child's capacity for competence. Mismanaged, it diminishes, deflates, and disables. And there is no in-between.

Resourcefulness: The capacity to find, invent, or adopt creative means of solving problems. This is the business, the very stuff of being human, isn't it? Homework provides the form (but not the *only* form); the child provides the substance. Assuming everyone can see past the report card, that is.

And to what, pray tell, do those Seven Hidden Values add? Why, to a belief in one's ability to deal adequately with adversity, which life is full of. That belief is what is usually called self-confidence, but I prefer to call it self-competence because people who have self-confidence believe they can succeed at anything. Those people, and this is backed by good research, don't deal well with failure. They often suffer emotional collapse—depression, anxiety, hopelessness—when they don't win. Much more functional is the feeling that one is capable of dealing *adequately* with adversity. Not that one will win but that one will walk away from the adverse experience having gained something, even if one lost. Therefore, homework provides children with the opportunity to develop that important attribute and, along with it, a sense of self-worth, which is what the first Seven Hidden Values add up to.

The manner in which the issue of homework is negotiated, managed, and otherwise handled within a family will set certain precedents that will influence how the child responds to future challenges, how the parents respond to future problems, and, most importantly, whether that child ever fully develops the skills he or she will need in order to establish and enjoy a successful adulthood.

So, for the kids' sake, let's get it right!

CHAPTER

3

Ending the Hassle

Tom Peters and Robert Waterman are two management consultants who wrote a widely read and widely praised book titled *In Search of Excellence* (Harper & Row, 1982). Although it dealt primarily with the issue of managing people in the workplace, *In Search of Excellence* applies to almost any situation in which one person is directing or teaching another. Interestingly enough, it is especially relevant to the raising of children.

Peters and Waterman make the point that the most effective managers are *consultants* to the people they manage. They are skilled at delegating responsibility and equally skilled at keeping a respectful distance from those to whom they delegate. They are authority figures who make their knowledge and expertise available to the people they supervise, but they do not hover over them, watching their every move.

Effective managers trust that the people they manage can do their jobs properly, and they communicate that trust by not becoming overly involved in their work. They motivate people by gently pushing the limits of their capacity for competence and self-direction. In so doing, they offer them the opportunity to discover the intrinsic rewards of independent achievement.

The consultant–manager's general policy is one of noninterference, and he breaks with this rule only if absolutely necessary. Likewise, where homework is concerned, a parent's proper role is that of *consultant* as opposed to *participant,* and a fine line divides one from the other. Upon crossing that line, parents step into emotional quicksand, and in the ensuing struggles, they sink deeper and deeper.

Parents who participate in the getting-done of homework not only dilute whatever academic learning was intended but also, and more importantly, enable the child to become dangerously dependent on their continued presence and help where homework is concerned.

The parent–consultant stands on the sidelines, providing encouragement and support.

The parent–participant runs on and off the field, scooping up the child's every fumble. He might even take the ball away if the child so much as looks like he's about to fumble. Little does the parent–participant realize, but he's actually *causing* the child to fumble. He serves as a constant distraction, and his interference prevents the child from ever feeling confident with the ball.

The parent–consultant is concerned but detached. He doesn't refuse any reasonable request for assistance, but his interventions are brief, rarely lasting more than a few minutes. One such intervention might be to refer the child's question back to the teacher—a subtle way of reinforcing the teacher's role as final authority where schoolwork is concerned.

The parent–participant, on the other hand, is so emotionally involved in the child's academic career that she winds up appropriating large chunks of it. The child's success or failure as a student confirms her success or failure as a parent, or so she thinks. In effect, the parent–participant is in there pitching for herself first and the child second.

It stands to reason: The more responsibility a parent assumes for homework, the less the child will assume. The more help a parent provides, the more helpless the child will feel. The harder a parent works to protect a child from failure, the more the child will begin to feel and act like a failure. After all, you don't need to be protected from failure unless you are in danger of failing, do you?

Instead of taking credit when their children do well in school and feeling guilt when they don't, parent–consultants *assign* their children responsibility, both positive and negative, for their own academic achievements and failures. Above all, they allow their children to make mistakes, realizing that the most valuable lessons in life are often learned by trial and error.

In all these ways, parent–consultants send messages of trust, affirmation, and personal worth to their children, who are, as a consequence, free to explore and expand their capacity for competence and creativity.

Parent–participants, although well intentioned, are overly involved in their children's lives. They live *through* their children and thus take their children's successes and failures very seriously and very personally. They overdirect, overprotect, and overindulge. They take on responsibility that rightfully belongs to their children, thus unintentionally robbing them of opportunities for growth.

The following chart contrasts these two roles, that of the overly involved parent–participant with the appropriately involved parent–consultant. Although we're talking specifically about homework, this chart applies to almost any area of a child's life: social, recreational, extracurricular, as well as academic. Ask yourself, "How does it apply to me?"

WHICH PARENT ARE YOU?

Parent–Participant	Parent–Consultant
Hovers, trying to prevent the child from making mistakes	Available, but allows the child to experience frustration and go through trial-and-error
Assumes responsibility that rightfully belongs to the child (lack of parent–child boundary)	Assigns responsibility to the child (parent–child boundary is in place)
Fosters dependence	Fosters independent, self-competent spirit
Unwittingly sends negative messages	Sends implicit positive messages

First, the overly involved parent–participant *hovers* over the child, obsessively preoccupied with the possibility that the child may make a mistake and determined to anticipate and prevent that unthinkable possibility. I call this "parenting by helicopter."

In the act of hovering, the parent–participant assumes responsibility, however unwittingly, for the child's academic (or social or recreational or extracurricular) decisions and performance. He overdirects, overmanages, and overcontrols. This is overprotection in its purest form—trying to protect the child from failure and one's self from the implication that the child's failure is a reflection of one's own.

Note that the parent–consultant is simply *available*—there to provide help when help is truly needed—but does not impose his presence on the child. In the non-act of being available, the parent–consultant assigns responsibility to the child for his own decisions and performance. Keep in mind that the more responsibility one is made to accept, the more responsible that person will eventually become. Note that the reverse is equally true.

In the act of hovering, the parent–participant encourages continuing *dependence*, weakens the child's tolerance for frustration, and thwarts the growth of initiative and resourcefulness. What a terrible price for a child to pay because a parent only wants to help her child do his best.

In the non-act of being simply and cleanly available, the parent–consultant encourages *independence* and all the things that go with it, including self-reliance, initiative, self-motivation, and resourcefulness.

In the act of hovering, the overly involved parent sends a powerful set of *negative messages*. These include, "I don't trust you to do an adequate job of this on your own," "I doubt that you're even capable of doing this on your own," and "You make me look bad and feel bad when you make mistakes." These are not the intended messages, but they are the felt messages, nonetheless; they are felt deep in the child's psyche, where they grow into feelings of incompetence, helplessness, and guilt. Eventually, they begin to affect nearly everything the child attempts. The child may even stop attempting anything at all in a desperate effort to stop the messages from doing their dirty work.

In the non-act of being simply available, the parent–consultant sends an equally powerful set of *positive messages,* including, "You are competent to do this on your own; I trust that you can, I trust that you want to, and I trust that you will." That also lodges itself deep within the child's psyche, where it shines and shines and shines and shines, lighting the way for one accomplishment after another.

The ABCs of Effective Homework Management

Are you convinced yet? Are you ready to extricate yourself from the never-ending, self-defeating, viciously circular trap of participating in your child's homework and get on with the joys—yes, the joys!—of consulting? Are you ready to get out of the homework business? Then read on, because it's as easy as A-B-C!

"A" Stands for "All by Myself"

The child does his homework in a private, personal place, preferably at a desk in his room, rather than in a public, family place such as the kitchen table. This physical arrangement not only helps define homework as the child's responsibility (one of the Seven Hidden Values of Homework) but also helps parents resist the urge to hover. As they say, "Out of sight, out of mind."

Homework done in the kitchen or any other family area quickly becomes a family affair. This virtually guarantees that homework will become a central, if not *the* central, issue in the family for most of the evening. Homework will command family attention, distract family members from more important responsibilities (such as being married), and drain energy from the family that might otherwise be available for more creative, productive pursuits (such as communication).

The child who is allowed to do homework at the kitchen table is being handed an opportunity to exercise a unique sort of control over the family. He sits in a position of power, at the center of a potential hurricane that he can set to swirling simply by acting incompetent. And once a child accidentally discovers what havoc he can cause and how much attention he can garner simply by acting incompetent, he will act incompetent more and more often. This behavior is not a manipulation, mind you. The child doesn't *want* to be incompetent; he doesn't want to pay this price. It's that he hasn't learned how to resist the temptation. In the process, the child becomes increasingly convinced that he is, in fact, incompetent and that he does need his parents' constant assistance to do homework. Furthermore, the attention the child receives is quite literally addicting. The more he gets, the more he thinks he needs, the more he wants. And since the only way to get it (or so he thinks) is to act helpless, he acts increasingly helpless. So, off to his room he goes!

The parents' first responsibility with regard to this personal, private homework place is to see to it that it's stocked with everything the child needs to do his homework on his own. In other words, it should be self-contained. There should be an ample supply of paper, pencils, and pens, a ruler, glue, tape, and—as they become necessary—a compass, protractor, and dictionary. A junior high or high school child's desk might even incorporate an L-shaped extension for a computer and printer. The child should be able to do his homework without ever leaving the security of his cozy little homework place. This promotes autonomy, another of homework's Seven Hidden Values.

The parents' second responsibility is to see to it that the child's homework place is comfortable. There should be a comfortable chair, one that provides good support to the lower back, and a desk compatible with the child's height. The desk should be no less than eighteen inches deep by three feet wide. This provides enough surface area for the child to spread out and work on fairly big projects. Needless to say, the child's desk should have its own lamp, preferably one on a goose-neck or swinging arm so it can be positioned directly over the work being done.

"B" Stands for "Back Off"

The child asks you to get involved. This means that you do not ask unnecessary questions like, "Do you need any help with your homework?" or "How can you do homework with that music playing?" or even "Do you have any homework today?" Furthermore, you don't do unnecessary things like checking to make sure the child is really doing his homework. Not only don't you offer help, you don't rush to the child's rescue if you hear him pounding his desk in frustration. Remember the value of things learned the hard way.

Now, this is not to say that you shouldn't *ever* help, because you can, but only if the child asks. This exercises initiative, yet another of homework's Seven Hidden Values. Likely as not, however, the child will not ask for help from his room nearly as often as he would ask if he were seated at the kitchen table.

When Willie and I implemented these homework management strategies with our two children, Eric and Amy, we also made a rule that if one of them had a question, he or she had to pick up books, paper, or whatever, and travel downstairs to where we were. "We will not come running upstairs at your beck and call," we told them. In other words, the effort involved in getting help belonged completely to the children. Amazing! The average number of requests for help per evening immediately dropped by more than half. This meant the children were putting more effort into any given problem before asking for help. This meant that perseverance—yet another of the Seven Hidden Values—was being exercised and therefore strengthened.

If the child asks for help, and the request is legitimate, then parents can and should give help. When they do, it should be for only one of two reasons: because the child is stuck at some point, has given it his all, and truly needs adult guidance to get unstuck or because he has finished his homework but wants someone to critique (check) it. In either instance, parents should limit their involvement to:

- *Clarifying* or reinterpreting directions
- *Demonstrating* or giving an example of a particular procedure
- *Reviewing* or checking work for accuracy, clarity, and adequacy

Whatever help is rendered should be *brief* and *encouraging*. Parental involvement should rarely last longer than ten minutes, with the norm being closer to five. If it looks like ten minutes isn't going to do it, then the parents should consider referring the problem back to the child's teacher, yes, *even if that means the child might not complete the work on time.*

If you decide to get involved, observe the following three rules:

Don't provide the child with a shortcut, which simply means you don't do the child's work for him. If he complains that he can't do the work on his own, that's an appropriate time to say, "Well, ask your teacher to explain this to you again and perhaps even give you some individual help during or after school."

In so many words, you're saying, "Perhaps you need to pay better attention in class. At the very least, you need to ask necessary questions of your teacher *before* you leave school. I'm not here to do *your* work for you or *her* work for her. If you truly can't, then put the work away. It will wait until tomorrow."

When our two children first began hearing this message from us, it had a curious effect. They complained, they cried, they even accused us of not caring whether they passed or failed, but more often—much more often—than not, the work got done before school the next day. They said, "We can't," to which we replied, "Well, we won't," and suddenly they could. And I've heard the same thing from a great many parents.

Don't get in over your head, which means you don't go back to school for the child's sake. If the child brings work to you that looks Greek to you, don't bang your head against the book trying to learn the subject matter. In other words, don't try to be a hero. Nine out of ten times, your best attempts to do so will only succeed in frustrating you along with your child. This is also an appropriate time to refer the child back to his teacher.

Don't get involved in an emotional exchange with your child over homework. If you decide to give help, and your child begins to complain that your explanation isn't clear or you aren't doing such-and-such the way the teacher said to do it, then just say, "Well, I guess that means I'm not the person to be helping you with this. Maybe you should call one of the other kids in the class and ask if they'll explain it to you. If that doesn't work, then I suppose you can always wait until tomorrow and ask your teacher to help you understand it." In other words, you always have the option of refusing to help your child with homework. It's amazing how motivating such a refusal can be, as the following story about my daughter, Amy, illustrates.

Upon entering the tenth grade, Amy was invited into advanced geometry. It was her first accelerated placement in math, and it turned out to be intimidating, at least initially.

The very first night of the new school year, Amy brought her geometry homework to me and, looking quite exasperated, asked for my help. Having been a rather good geometry student in my day and, like most doting dads, unable to pass up an opportunity to impress my daughter, I spent about thirty minutes refamiliarizing myself with the material and showing her how to work the problems. As understanding dawned, the lines of tension disappeared from her face, and when I finished she gave me a hug and a warm, "Thank you, Daddy."

Bill Cosby, you ain't got nothin' on me, I thought.

The next night, Amy again brought her geometry homework to me, and again I earned a smile and a hug. This scene repeated itself almost every night for the first two weeks of school. I finally woke up to the fact that Amy was leaning increasingly on me to relieve her frustrations over geometry and that in the long run, my helpfulness wasn't doing her any favors.

So the next night, when she once again approached me, geometry book in hand, I said, "Amy, I've decided not to give you any more help with geometry, at least not for a while. I think I've helped you get off to a good start, and I'm certain you can handle it pretty much on your own from here."

Her face fell, and she stared at me in disbelief. "Daddy," she pleaded, "I've tried to figure it out, and I can't!"

"Well," I replied, "I think you can. They wouldn't have offered an advanced math class to you if they didn't think you could handle it."

"But Daddy, everyone's having problems in there. Nobody understands it!"

"Then that's something all of you need to call to your teacher's attention. If you don't understand the material, you can ask your teacher for extra help, or you can ask a student who *does* understand it to explain it to you. But the bottom line, Amy, is that your daddy's not going to take geometry this year."

She gave me a look that would kill and then, with tears welling up in her eyes, ran from the room, à la Sarah Bernhardt. Pausing at the bottom of the stairs, she dramatically announced, "Then I'll just *fail* geometry!"

When that got no reaction, she ran upstairs and, pausing once again on the landing, cried out, "You'd have helped Eric!"

Ah, yes, I should have known. If all else fails, try the old you've-always-liked-him-better routine.

One of the things parenthood has taught me is that you don't necessarily do children any favors by trying to make them happy. I could have continued to cooperate and relieve Amy's anguish over geometry. In fact, that would have been the *easiest* thing to do. Instead, I withdrew my support before she became overly dependent on it. That forced her to exercise her powers of perseverance and, therefore, strengthen them.

In so doing, I made her very unhappy. I'm sure that for a time at least, she hated me for it, but then parenthood isn't a popularity contest, and children tend to be very dramatic. Sometimes, in order to promote a child's progress toward self-sufficiency, parents must do highly unpopular things.

I've also learned that it's possible for a parent to say something positive and affirming to a child and for the child to not like it at all. In this case, I sent Amy a set of very complimentary messages, including "you're competent," "you're smart," and "you can do it on your own." Nonetheless, I upset her greatly.

She wanted me to say, in effect, "You're absolutely right. You do need my help. You can't do this on your own." Needless to say, even though it would have been unintentional, that would have been the worst possible message to send. If you paddle someone else's canoe long enough, they not only never learn to paddle it themselves, they also become convinced that only *you* are capable of paddling it.

Many of today's parents are reluctant to do anything that causes their children even temporary unhappiness. There are three factors at work here: first, the mistaken belief that unhappiness threatens a child's self-esteem; second, the fear that their children will feel unloved or—horror of horrors—won't like them; and third, the fear that teachers and other parents will disapprove of their child-rearing methods.

So they get into lockstep with the crowd and dedicate themselves to the popular cause of keeping their children happy, no matter what the cost. In the process, they unwittingly deprive their children of opportunities to develop essential feelings of self-competence. What these parents fail to realize is that it's often necessary to temporarily threaten a child's happiness in order to promote a lasting reward.

Oh, yes, about Amy. She must have discovered the joys of paddling her own canoe, because despite the fact that she never again asked for my help, she made straight A's in geometry that year.

"C" Stands for "Create Limits"

Two important limits should be set for homework involvement. First, as I did with Amy in the previous story, parents should set a limit on how much homework help they are willing to provide. Second, parents should set a limit on how late a child can work on homework. We'll take these one at a time.

Set a limit on homework help. Whenever I talk to parents or teachers about school issues, I always get around to asking two questions.

- ◆ "True or false: When a child comes to you and says he needs help with an academic problem, you should help." Everyone answers true. I can't remember anyone ever saying that that statement is false.

- ◆ Then, after everyone has given the wrong answer, I ask, "True or false: Probably 80 percent of the time on average, when a child says he needs help with a problem, he doesn't really need help at all. He is simply not willing to expend the energy or time necessary to solve the problem (in other words, he's asking for help because he's lazy) or has reached the limits of his tolerance for frustration concerning the problem." And everyone gives me the right answer.

Thus I establish that just because children *say* they need help doesn't mean they really do. It's the job of parents and teachers to give help when needed, not simply when wanted. When a person helps someone else who was capable of solving the problem himself, the helper wasn't really doing the helpee any favors. In that situation, the helper was an enabler, and enabling always, without exception, weakens the person being helped.

With this in mind, set an upper limit on the amount of homework help you will give on any given evening (or nonschool day). Use the 20 percent rule to determine that limit. If your child is asking about ten homework questions a night, then the limit should be two. Communicate the new limit this way: "From now on, I am only going to answer or give help with two homework questions or problems per night. Finish everything you can do on your own, then figure out what two questions or problems you need the most help with and bring them to me. I will spend no more than fifteen minutes on the two problems. After fifteen minutes, if you still don't get it, that simply means I am not able to give you good help in which case you need to take those problems to your teacher the next day."

I've been making this recommendation for many years and have had lots of parents sign on. Every single time a parent gives me feedback, it sounds like this: "For a week or so my son had difficulty with the new rule. He would beg me for more help beyond the two-question limit. A couple of times he even cried and told me I was mean. Then, after that week or two, he accepted the rule. He would do his homework—what he could do on his own—and then bring me two problems. That happened for maybe a month. Then, he began bringing me only one problem a night. That lasted a month. Now, he rarely brings me a problem, but the amazing thing is, John—and you told me this would happen—his grades have improved considerably!"

A great example of when less is actually more!

Set an upper time limit on homework. In most instances, the child should be responsible for deciding when to begin, but parents should decide when to call "time." The deadline should be consistent, say eight o'clock every evening, but it can be temporarily suspended for special projects and when the child needs more time to study for major tests. The shortest route to a nightly homework marathon is to tell a child when to begin but not when he must be done. Setting an upper limit teaches time management, another of homework's Seven Hidden Values. Since I told a story about Amy, it's only fair that I now tell one about her brother.

Eric is the older of our two children, and when he was in the fourth grade, his bedtime was nine o'clock. Supposedly, that is, because about a month into the school year, he devised a clever way of managing to stay up later. When we told him it was time to start getting ready for bed, he would suddenly remember homework that was due the next day.

"How could you forget?" we would ask.

"I don't know," he'd say, "I just did."

"Okay, Eric, but make it snappy."

And the lights in Eric's room would stay on until ten or even eleven o'clock, with us going to his room every fifteen minutes or so asking, "How much longer is this going to take?" and him answering, "I'm almost done."

Finally, after this had gone on for a couple of weeks, Willie and I finally figured out the game and made a rule that he had to finish his homework—regardless how much of it there was—by eight o'clock.

"Eight o'clock is when we all put our responsibilities down, whatever they are, and become a family again," we said. "We're not going to do office work or housework after eight o'clock, and you're not going to do homework.

"If you have a big test or a major project due the next day and you feel you need more time than the deadline allows, you must let one of us know and ask for an extension as soon as you get home from school. If you forget to ask or don't realize you need to ask until later, the answer will be 'No.'"

"Okay! Okay!" he said, which is what they always say.

The next day, Eric brought some books home but played outside with friends until supper. After supper, he went upstairs to do homework, or so we thought. At eight o'clock, I went up to his room to find him working on a model.

"Hey, big guy," I said, "Mom and I would like you to come downstairs for a while before you start getting ready for bed."

"Oh, wow!" he exclaimed, "What time is it?"

"Eight o'clock," I answered.

"Oh, wow! I lost track of time. I've got some homework to do!"

"Oh, wow!" I said, "I guess you're out of luck."

"Why?" he asked, as if he didn't know.

"Because we made a rule, Eric, and that's the way it's going to be."

"But I forgot!"

"That's exactly why we made the rule, Eric."

"But Dad, I'll get a zero if I don't have my homework done!"

"So be it, Eric. Now come downstairs and spend some time with us."

"Dad!"

"Dad me no dads, Eric. Come downstairs."

"Okay! I'll be down in a minute."

Knowing full well what Eric's next move in this cat-and-mouse game was going to be, I went downstairs, waited a few minutes, took off my shoes, tiptoed back up to his room, and opened the door. He looked up from his desk, where he was working on arithmetic problems.

"Give me your books, Eric," I said.

"Aw, Dad, you gotta be kidding," he whined, "I gotta finish this before school tomorrow!"

"Right, and you can get yourself up early in the morning and do it. Or when you get to school instead of socializing with your friends, you can find a quiet place in the cafeteria and do these problems. Or you can tell your teacher that the reason you don't have your homework done is because your parents are mean and slightly crazy to boot and wouldn't let you do it, but you're giving me your books right now and coming downstairs."

"Dad, please," he pleaded, "I just forgot. I'll remember tomorrow, I promise."

"No. Give me the books."

Reluctantly, he handed over the books. The next morning, I heard his alarm clock go off at six o'clock. I heard him go downstairs and into the kitchen; then he came back upstairs and closed his door. That night, I went to his room at eight o'clock. He was hunched over a writing assignment.

"Time to put the homework away, Eric."

"Dad, I've got to finish this report. It's taking longer than I thought it would. Then I've got a spelling test to study for, but I'll be in bed by nine, I promise."

"Eric?"

"What, Dad?"

"Give me the books."

"Dad, no, I mean, I can't, I mean, it's not fair, Dad, really, c'mon Dad, please. PLEASE?"

"No."

He ranted. He raved. He gave me the books but refused to come downstairs. He went to bed at nine o'clock. The next morning, I heard his alarm go off at six. Again, I heard him go down to the kitchen then back upstairs, closing his door.

The next night, he had his homework done at eight o'clock. But that wasn't the end of it. Over the next few weeks, Eric tested the new rule, as any child would, in a number of brilliantly creative ways. And every time, I simply said, "Give us the books."

At last, convinced that I meant what I said, Eric fell into a consistent routine of getting his homework done, believe it or not, *well before* eight o'clock. He'd come home, change clothes, and go outside until supper, after which he'd retire to his room. He'd usually emerge around seven or seven-thirty. If he had more homework than usual, he'd start on it immediately after school and sometimes be done before supper. In any case, I never again had to confiscate his books at eight o'clock. Meanwhile, he passed Introduction to Time Management 101 with flying colors!

Darrell Learns That He Can!

I once passed on my homework management plan to the parents of a fourth-grade boy whom I'll call Darrell. Darrell had previously been successful at getting his mother to sit through homework with him nearly every night. Predictably, a homework marathon had developed and was consuming the family's evenings.

Complicating matters was the fact that Darrell had been diagnosed as having a learning disability and spent an hour a day in a special education program. This only reinforced his parents' belief that he needed lots of help with his studies. Therefore, Mom viewed her nightly sacrifice as absolutely essential. She was convinced that without her support, Darrell would suffer a total academic collapse. Needless to say, persuading these folks to implement the ABCs of my homework management program was no small act of salesmanship.

But they did. They set an upper limit of eight o'clock and, slowly but surely, became occasional consultants rather than full-time participants. After some initial displays of helplessness, Darrell began doing his homework pretty much on his own, in his room rather than at the kitchen table as before. At eight, whether he was finished or not, his parents made him put his books aside and prepare for his nine o'clock bedtime. Within several weeks, his teachers reported that not only was Darrell turning in all his homework and completing more work in school but that the quality of his work was improving.

Although Mom was much less involved, she continued the practice of calling out Darrell's spelling words on Thursday night, in preparation for Friday's test.

"Is this okay?" she asked during one of our conversations.

I pointed out that as an alternative she could purchase an inexpensive cassette recorder and teach Darrell how to make a review tape of each week's spelling words. This would make him more responsible and more independent, and he might actually do better in spelling.

"I know," his mother said, "but I *like* reading him the spelling words. It makes me feel like I'm doing *something*."

"Then it's okay by me, as long as you enforce the rules otherwise," I said. That was that, until a month or so later when she told this tale. One Thursday night, Darrell started watching television after supper and was still watching at eight o'clock. Suddenly, realizing what time it was, he panicked. He jumped up, ran to his room, got his spelling book, and asked his mother to give him his practice test. Mom refused, pointing out that homework time was over. Darrell was beside himself and insisted that he would surely fail the next day's test, and it would be her fault.

"It was hard," she said, recounting the incident. "There was a whole hour before his bedtime that I could have helped him, but I didn't."

"So what did he do?" I asked.

"Well, the next morning he got up early and studied his words by himself in his room. Then he went to school and used the half-hour between when the bus gets him to school and the first bell to study some more. It was the first time he'd studied them all on his own."

"So how'd he do on the test?" I asked.

"You won't believe this," his mother said, laughing. "He got the first perfect score he'd ever gotten on a spelling test."

In truth, I had no trouble believing it at all. It never fails: The more responsible a child is for his or her school performance, the better the child does in school.

How Much Homework Is Enough?

One of the more unfortunate things that the never-ending rollout of "education reform" has spawned is an overemphasis on *quantity* where homework is concerned. The following letter, sent to me by the parents of two elementary-age children, illustrates the problem: "The school our children attend places a great deal of emphasis on homework. Teachers begin assigning homework in the last half of kindergarten, and it builds from there. It isn't unusual for a third-grade child to average two hours of homework a night, four nights a week. And that's two hours, mind you, only if the child doesn't dawdle."

An unfortunate situation but not at all uncommon. In 1983, a presidential commission report on education called ours a "nation at risk." In response, many school systems across the nation embraced the work ethic. In their obsessive zeal to improve their rankings in the standardized test scores game, they made the mistake of thinking that more is better.

Presumably, the thinking is that learning and retention take place in direct proportion to the amount of time a child spends practicing a given lesson. In fact, there is a grain of truth in that, but the point of diminishing returns is reached quickly. Studies show that when someone is learning a large amount of new information or a new skill, it's best to separate the total learning time into several brief practice periods. This is known as "distributive practice" or "distributive learning." In contrast, "massed practice" occurs when learning is expected to take place in one large chunk of time. Assigning fifty division problems when ten would suffice is an example of massed practice.

A major problem with massed practice is that too many learning trials tend to produce an aversive response toward the learning itself. Aversive conditioning results in attempts by the learner to avoid the cause of his or her discomfort.

If the learner is a child and the discomfort is caused by excessive homework, avoidance behaviors will include putting it off 'til the last minute, lying about it, acting incompetent, finding numerous excuses to wander off task, staring out the window, and trying to get someone else to shoulder part, if not all, of the load. In short, that's the very set of problems that make up the homework hassle.

In addition, too much homework can result in a child eventually losing interest in school and motivation for learning altogether. I don't need to tell you that this is the deepest cut of all.

Research on human learning strongly suggests that although homework is a worthwhile exercise, it should not demand much more than thirty minutes per day on average, especially during the early elementary grades. (I recommend that homework be introduced in the second half of first grade.) Any more than this and returns are likely to diminish. For a fourth-, fifth-, and sixth-grade child, homework should not consume more than sixty minutes a day.

This makes good common sense from a practical standpoint as well. Six hours spent in school and one hour spent on homework amounts to a seven-hour academic day. Considering that an eight-hour workday is standard for adults, seven hours is plenty to expect of a twelve-year-old child.

From seventh grade on, the heat can be gradually increased. Most high school students, and especially those on a college-prep track, should be able to tolerate an average of two hours of homework per night, occasionally more. At this point, the increased load begins to prepare youngsters for the more rigorous demands of college.

I Told You So!

In the largest-ever study of the relationship between parental involvement and child achievement, researchers at the University of Texas and Duke University analyzed three decades of data, including sixty-three measures of parent participation in children's academics. What they discovered confirmed what I've been saying since the mid-1980s: Parents who help with homework may actually be hurting their children's chances for success. That was the finding regardless of race, income, or education level. For example, parental homework help did not correlate with high scores on standardized tests and is likely to bring down a child's overall achievement. Right!

When parents help with homework, they are taking responsibility for the child's achievement level. It's really a very simple equation: The more responsible the parent, the less responsible the child. Furthermore, many kids whose parents help with homework develop what psychologists term "learned helplessness syndrome." The more the parents help, the more incompetent the children feel, and this is especially true for their academic studies. The truth is that struggle is not always a bad thing, and it can help the child grow and learn. The simple fact that a child is struggling does not justify having his parents jump in to "help." For readers who are interested, the entire study can be found in *The Broken Compass: Parental Involvement with Children's Education* by Keith Robinson and Angel L. Harris (Harvard University Press, 2014).

Questions?

Q *Doesn't a young child—a first grader, for example—who's never had experience with homework need more initial guidance and parental involvement than you're recommending?*

A Absolutely! Just as an employee needs more supervision and direction while phasing into a new job than he will eventually require, so the young child needs more guidance from parents while making the adjustment to having homework.

However, parents need to understand that the initial nature and extent of their involvement in homework will set a precedent. Parents who become overly involved from the first will find it difficult to eventually reduce that involvement, but parents who are initially conservative in their involvement will have little problem gradually pulling back.

The first of my Homework ABCs doesn't change. Regardless of the child's age or level of experience with homework, homework should be confined to the child's room or some other private place. This makes it clear, from the first, that homework is the child's responsibility, not a family affair.

The second and third of those ABCs change slightly. A homework deadline should be established and enforced from the start. But the young child is going to need more structure than a deadline alone will provide. This can be done in one of two ways:

* Shortly after the child arrives home, parent and child take a few moments to make an inventory of the child's homework assignments. Taking after-school activities and other factors into consideration, the parent should help the child decide when he needs to begin in order to finish before the

established deadline. This simple exercise helps the child begin learning how to manage time, which is, again, one of homework's Seven Hidden Values.

◆ The parent sets a consistent time for starting homework and a deadline. The actual amount of time should be no more than enough to allow the child to finish before the deadline on the heaviest of homework days. Although this approach isn't quite as effective as the previous one at helping the child to learn time management skills, the routine may be more convenient for some families.

Regardless of how it's determined, when the decided-upon homework time rolls around, the young child is probably going to need a gentle reminder: "It's seven o'clock, Heathcliff. Does that mean something to you?"

After the youngster retires to his or her homework place, parents should check in every so often to see how things are coming along. Their involvement, if any, should be brief and encouraging. As it approaches, they should also remind the child of the deadline. When it arrives, they should enforce it.

Q *If parents have been having problems with homework management, and they implement your Homework ABCs, how long should they expect to wait until things begin working?*

A My experience has been that, generally speaking, five out of ten homework-resistant children will begin rehabilitating themselves three or four weeks after their parents implement the plan. The actual length of time is a function of how dependent the child has become on parental participation in the homework. If it's still early in the game, and not much dependency has been established, then the child may pick up the ball and run with it almost immediately. If the child has had time to become very dependent on parental participation, then it's probably going to take several weeks before things begin turning around. During that time, parents should expect things to get worse before they start getting better.

After parents stop compensating for the child's homework problems and assign responsibility for them to the child, the child will test to see whether they really mean what they say. He asks himself, "Are they really going to go through with it? Are they really going to put it all in my lap, or are they just blowing so much hot air, like they've done so often in the past?"

Once he has tested his parents' resolve for a couple of weeks and discovered that they really do intend to give him complete responsibility for the homework, then the child must make a critical decision. He must choose between success and failure, between whether he wants to do well in school or not. The choice is now his and his alone, which it's never been before. Because it's new and therefore intimidating, he may have to wrestle with it for a while before making a decision. During this decisive struggle, expect the child to act like he's desperately in need of rescue. In other words, expect things to get worse. Given a choice between success and failure, most people will choose success. And after three or four weeks of wrestling and acting like they're going to sink rather than swim, most children with major homework problems make the correct choice. They'll begin swimming.

Q *What if the child doesn't make the correct choice? What if, after three or four weeks, it looks like he's choosing failure? What should parents do then?*

A After the parents invite the problem out into the open, if it gets worse and shows no sign of taking a turn for the better, then one of two things is going on.

First possibility: So much dependency has accumulated that the child is unable to discharge it on his own. In that case, the parents will have to jump-start the child's motivational motor. In other words, they will have to take the bull by the horns and manage the child toward making the correct decision. There are ways of managing children toward making correct, success-oriented decisions without assuming responsibility for their inappropriate behavior. In Chapter 4 I'll discuss some of those techniques and give examples of how they can be used to help the problem student. But be patient; we'll get there in a few pages.

Second possibility: There's more to the problem than meets the eye, meaning the child has a problem or problems that need professional attention—tutoring, for example. That's the subject of Chapter 4 also.

Q *My eight-year-old is now in second grade, and she has needed my help with homework since she started school. At first, it was just occasional, but as the work became more difficult, her needs increased to the point that my help is now almost constant. I agree that under ideal circumstances parents should be a few steps removed from a child's homework, but certainly there are exceptions. For example, if I were not so involved, my daughter would certainly fail the second grade. Don't you agree it would be irresponsible of me to simply let this happen?*

A Not necessarily. There's a lot to be said for letting the chips fall where they may in situations of this sort. I think I understand your dilemma. You don't want your daughter to fail in the sense of having to repeat the second grade. You probably think that failure would damage her psyche. Your sense of responsibility demands that you do everything within your power to prevent that from happening.

Without realizing it, however, you're digging an ever-deepening hole for both yourself and your daughter. The longer you dig, the harder it's going to be to climb out, and the greater the cost of trying to do so.

You worry that if you stop helping her with homework, she will fail. For the moment, I'm going to accept your terminology and acknowledge that you may be right. The question is, *are you really preventing your daughter from failure, or are you just forestalling the inevitable*? If your daughter is unable to do second-grade work, then perhaps a tutor is called for, or it might be in her best interest to repeat second grade. In any case, having you effectively go to second grade for her won't solve the problem. What you're doing is accelerating rapidly toward an inevitable collision with what I call the Sooner or Later Principle. A debt is accumulating, and sooner or later, it will have to be repaid.

It's conceivable that with enough effort you can get your daughter all the way through high school and into college. Who's going to help her with homework then? Will you hire a full-time tutor to accompany her to her classes and see that she gets a degree? Then who will make sure she succeeds in her chosen career? If you want your daughter to learn to stand on her own two feet instead of always looking around for another pair to stand on, then perhaps you need to let her fail.

Failing a grade and feeling like a failure are two entirely different things, although they are often confused even by educators. One does not necessarily follow from the other. It's possible for a child to never repeat a grade and end up feeling like a failure. It's equally possible for a child to repeat a grade and end up feeling like a winner.

Indeed, your daughter's sense of self-competence is at stake. The more help you give, the more dependent on your help she becomes. The more dependent she becomes, the more incapable and inadequate she feels. The more inadequate she feels, the worse she feels about herself, the further her self-esteem falls. The further it falls, the more helpless she will act, and the more she will look toward you to prop her up.

If you really want to help your daughter, have a psychologist test her to determine the reasons behind her school performance problems and develop a prescriptive remedial plan. It's entirely possible that the problem can be corrected without your daughter repeating the second grade. Then again, it may be that retention would be in her very best interests at this point. In either case, you need to get out of the homework business and let the chips fall where they may. If you don't, sooner or later there's going to be a rude awakening.

Q *Our children's teachers frequently assign projects that the children can't possibly do without parental help. We don't mind providing occasional assistance, but we feel that the extent of our involvement defeats the purpose of these projects. On the other hand, if we don't help, the child will not receive a good grade and as a result will almost certainly suffer humiliation and perhaps even ridicule from other students. What do you suggest?*

A I wholeheartedly agree that too much parental participation in projects defeats the purpose of the projects themselves, which should be to give children the opportunity to learn how to synthesize a number of smaller learning experiences into a larger whole, establish and pursue long-range goals, and experience the rewards of independent accomplishment. All of this becomes diluted, if not eradicated, when parents become overly involved.

Teachers have no business assigning work that children can't do, for the most part, on their own. Those who do need to be gently reminded that one of the purposes of education is to help outfit children for responsible self-sufficiency. When I was in school, it was made clear that parents were *not* to help with projects. If it was obvious that a child had received parental help, his grade was docked. Today, it's taken for granted that parents are supposed to help, and teachers will reward the children whose parents got involved with better grades. This upside-down practice means, in effect, that children who do their projects on their own are punished for exercising initiative and independence and resourcefulness. That makes no sense.

So what can you do as a parent? For starters, you can discuss the issue with other parents and perhaps even bring it up at a parent-teacher meeting. You and several other parents could form an ad hoc committee to do research on the issue of homework and make recommendations to the school about quantity and the advisability of assigning projects that require parental participation.

If you have the courage, you could stop giving your children much help with their projects. You could limit your involvement to consulting and advising but keep your hands clean of the actual doings. That may mean that your children don't get excellent ratings on their projects, in which case you should tell them in advance that the grade isn't that important. Tell them that what's important is for them to do their projects pretty much on their own, that they do their best, and that they take pride in what they've done, even if it doesn't win an award.

When we pulled out of our children's projects, we told them, "This may mean that you don't get an excellent grade. It may mean that your project isn't chosen for the science fair. That's certainly not fair, but that's the way things may turn out. But we want you to know that if you do a project on your own and you do your best, then regardless of the grade your teacher gives you, you get an Excellent from us."

From that point on, whenever they finished a major project, we took them out to the eatery of their choice to celebrate their independent accomplishment.

Your direct involvement in your children's projects isn't, in the long run, in their best interest regardless of the grades they make. In the long run, your support and encouragement will mean a lot more to their growth and development than an A on a project they really didn't do.

Q *My daughter's kindergarten teacher recently started assigning homework. It really doesn't amount to much—just practice in forming letters and numbers, along with a page or two of coloring. Missy's problem is her dissatisfaction with her work. She doesn't make her numbers and letters well enough to suit herself and thinks her coloring is ugly. Consequently, she winds up doing everything over three or four times when her first attempt was perfectly okay. The more help and encouragement I provide, the madder at herself she becomes. At times, she's made statements like "I'm dumb" and "I can't do anything!" Her teacher sees none of this at school, however. In fact, she tells me Missy is one of the quickest learners in the class. How can I help her?*

A You can start by not helping her. Keep things in perspective. Missy is going through some fairly major changes right now. She's in school for the first time, and she's learning new skills. She's trying to please you, she's trying to please the teacher, she's trying to please herself. And on top of all that, she has homework to contend with. Understandably, she feels a fair amount of pressure.

The way you manage the homework situation will be precedent setting. In the final analysis, you want Missy to accept responsibility for her homework, set realistic goals for herself, and take pride in what she accomplishes. You certainly don't want her to become a neurotic little perfectionist at age five.

Two things are clear. First, you know she can do the work and do it well—the teacher has already assured you of that. Second, she doesn't get bent out of shape about her work in school. We also know that the teacher, with twenty-five or so other kids in the class, is unable to give Missy the amount of attention you can. Ah-ha! So now we know that the less attention Missy gets, the less pressure she feels, the better her attitude is toward herself, and the more calmly and competently she works.

Now you know what to do! Stop giving her so much attention. In other words, stop helping her. The solution lies in implementing the ABCs of my homework management system, as described earlier in this chapter. Missy should do her homework in her room, she should receive your help only if she asks for it and then only if you decide she truly needs it, and she should be expected to finish her homework by a reasonable hour, say seven o'clock. Establishing a homework deadline will limit her obsessing and prevent homework from becoming a marathon.

If she complains about her performance, just say, "Do what you think you need to do to get it right. Whatever you decide is fine with me. I love you and trust you to do your best."

Don't, under any circumstances, try to persuade her that her work is fine when she's insisting it isn't. Just say a few encouraging words and excuse yourself from the room. This puts the problem in her lap, where she can decide what she wants to do about it.

Without intending to do so, Missy has manufactured this problem. There isn't a shred of evidence that it exists outside her imagination. In effect, it's a soap opera, and she's the producer. When you stop being the audience, it will quickly go off the air.

Q *Like Missy, our second grader has become a perfectionist when it comes to his homework. He takes an inordinate amount of time forming and spacing his letters correctly and ends up* *erasing and starting over a lot because his first attempt doesn't suit him. Every Thursday night, I give him a practice spelling test, which is just about the only help he gets from me all week. I end up getting very frustrated with him because he takes so long to write each word. What should take ten minutes, at most, takes thirty. His teacher says he was doing similar stuff at the beginning of the school year, but he stopped when she put her foot down. When I put my foot down, however, all I get is a sore foot. Do you have a solution?*

A Yes, I do. In fact, I have not one but two solutions. You can't beat that, now can you?

First solution: Make a rule that he can take as much time as he wants to write each word but that you will read words for only fifteen minutes. When you start giving him his practice test, set a timer. When it rings, excuse yourself from the room, regardless of how many words there are left. As you leave, say, "I'm sure you can teach yourself the rest of these without me."

This forces him to make a crucial decision: Is it more important that he get through the list or that he write each word perfectly? This gives him an opportunity to experience and begin to profit from the all-important "You Can't Have Your Cake and Eat It Too" principle. I'll just bet that the first few times you do this, the timer will ring before you've finished the list. I'll also bet that his spelling test grades won't suffer a bit.

There's an even better solution, however. I'm sure you'd agree that teaching your son *how* to study on his own is preferable to helping him study. At present, although your intentions can't be faulted, you aren't really helping him develop good study skills. When parents help children with homework, especially when the help isn't necessary, children quickly become convinced they need the help. In other words, they become *dependent* on it. When they become dependent on the help, they begin doing things to perpetuate it, like taking thirty minutes to do something that should take only ten.

For parents, our single most important job is that of teaching our children to stand on their own two feet. It's called self-sufficiency or self-competence. The more children do for themselves on their own, the more competent they feel. The more competent they feel, the more they want to do on their own, the more competent they act, and so on.

Second (and better) solution: Buy your son a cassette recorder and a blank tape and show him how to make his own spelling test—he reads a word into the recorder, pauses long enough to write the word, spells the word into the recorder, pauses again, reads the next word, and so on. Now his obsessing affects him and no one else. That forces him to decide whether he really wants to obsess or not.

I bet I know what decision he'll make.

Q *At the beginning of the year, our daughter's first-grade teacher sent a note home to all the parents requesting that they have the children read to them for thirty minutes every night. We can understand the reasoning behind the request, but carrying it out has been nothing but a hassle. Five minutes into the exercise, Lisa's had enough. From that point on, we must prod and scold to get her to finish. Meanwhile, her pronunciation gets increasingly sloppy, and we get increasingly frustrated. All too often, the whole situation ends in tears. The real shame is that Lisa has always loved to have us read to her. Now, instead of being a joy, reading is fast becoming a drudge. Do you have any suggestions?*

A I sure am glad you asked, because yours is a tale familiar to thousands of other parents. All across America, children who once enjoyed having their parents read to them now dread reading to their parents. When the time comes, their reluctance emerges in the form of careless pronunciation, whining, and general dragging of feet (or eyeballs, as the case may be). Their parents might think they're just being lazy. But the problem lies not with the child but with the method.

Your daughter's teacher wants to accomplish a number of things with this nightly exercise. First, she wants the children to practice their reading skills at home. Second, she wants parents to become involved in their children's education. Third, she wants to keep parents abreast of their children's progress in reading. Fourth, she's probably hoping that the exercise is enjoyable for both parent and child, thereby increasing the child's motivation to read.

The teacher's purposes can't be faulted, but she's going about them in a counterproductive manner. In the first place, even given a better method, thirty minutes is much too long. At this age, a child's attention span for activities that require sitting in one spot and doing one thing is simply not that long. Remember also what I said earlier in this chapter about *massed* versus *distributed* practice. As you've discovered, the point of diminishing returns is reached very early in this particular game.

Game? Not really, and that's the second, bigger problem. It's no fun! There's no play or give-and-take, only pressure to perform for thirty straight and tedious minutes. If there's a better way to make a child hate reading, I haven't heard of it. So here are my suggestions:

- Reduce the time to *ten* minutes. Better yet, agree to stop at a certain point, such as after one or two stories. You might tell the teacher of your intentions and explain to her your reasons, but if she objects, remember that you don't need her permission.
- Let your daughter choose at least some of what's to be read, even if it turns out to be something she's read many times before and knows by heart.

- ❖ Instead of having your daughter read to you the entire time, take turns reading to one another. You read a page, she reads a page, and so on. You can even alternate sentence by sentence.

Concerning that last suggestion, studies have shown that an early elementary school–age child's reading skills will improve simply as a result of being read to by an adult. When you read to her, hold the book so she can see it and follow along. This helps her learn to begin scanning more rapidly. Gradually, her reading speed will improve. Last, but by no means least, it will be enjoyable. And any reading exercise that fails to accomplish that isn't worth the time.

Q *We've been using your homework management system with our second-grade daughter for the last year with much success. She does her homework on her own and asks us for help only occasionally. But after finishing her work, she does ask us to check it. If we understand you correctly, that's okay, but what should we do when we find mistakes? Should we point them out or be less specific and let her figure them out for herself?*

A Yes, checking a child's work is perfectly okay, as long as the *child* initiates the request, which is what your daughter is doing. How you deal with mistakes is a judgment call, meaning there is no absolute answer to your question. Sometimes, it's more appropriate to refer specifically to the mistake, saying, "You might want to give this problem some more thought." This is different from saying, "You need to redo this." In other words, just put the ball in the child's court and let her decide what she wants to do with it.

At other times, it's more appropriate to say, "You've made several errors on this page. They look like careless mistakes to me. I'm sure you'll catch them yourself if you go over the assignment one more time."

I lean toward the second option unless (a) the child was obviously tired or burned out on doing homework that evening; (b) the assignment was long, and going over it problem by problem would take a good deal of time (remember the pitfalls of mass practice); or (c) the mistake was an isolated one and nothing would be gained by having the child find it on her own.

In the final analysis, the answer to your question is that you should use your common sense.

Q *Our fourteen-year-old daughter likes to do her homework with her radio on, tuned to her favorite rock station. I don't see how she can do her best with that noise going in the background, but she says it doesn't bother her and she can't study without it. She maintains that as long as her grades are good (and they are) I have no right to interfere in how she does her homework. What do you think?*

A I agree completely with your daughter. When I was a teenager, I did my homework to the strains of Elvis, Buddy Holly, Dion and the Belmonts, and later, the Beatles and the Rolling Stones. Like you, my parents thought the music was a distraction. I always thought they objected more to my *selection* than to the idea of music in the background. Mozart would have been fine. After all, *he* was a genius. But they were convinced that Elvis was a degenerate and feared that too much exposure to his music would affect me likewise.

Actually, I think my grades were *better* because of rock 'n' roll. My English themes had rhythm, a backbeat. My math homework had symmetry. The music kicked me in the right side of my brain, unleashing my imagination, my sense of possibility, the power to see through the concrete to the abstract. A wop bop a lu bop, a wop bam boom!

Remember that a kid's brain isn't as cluttered as an adult's. It's no sweat for a teenager to listen to rock 'n' roll with one part of the brain, do homework with another part, and still chew gum! After all, kids can do just about anything better and faster than adults. They learn new languages faster, they figure out Rubik's Cube faster, and they master new electronic devices in the time it takes an adult to figure out how to turn them on.

The older and more congested the brain gets, the more of a distraction rock music becomes when you're doing things such as homework. After age thirty or so, you have to start listening to classical or new age music because that stuff stays in the background—it doesn't compete. Worse yet, we sometimes even talk ourselves into thinking we like it.

A number of years ago, I was surprised to learn from a surgeon friend that operating rooms are equipped with expensive stereo systems and that most operations are performed to the surgeon's favorite tunes. My friend's tastes ran to rhythm and blues from the fifties and sixties. "Some of my best cuts," he once told me, "were made while I was listening to Otis Redding."

"Loud?" I asked.

"Is there any other way?" he answered with a grin.

I had this vision of doctors and nurses boogalooing around the O.R. to relieve the tension of the life-and-death matters they're dealing with.

I agree with your daughter. As long as her grades are good, how she does her homework is none of your business. So let the little girl rock!

Q *Almost every time my nine-year-old son, who's in the third grade, asks me to explain a homework problem to him, he gets upset either because he doesn't understand the explanation or because I don't do the problem the way his teacher wants it done. I find myself explaining over and over again, while he gets more and more upset. Finally, I reach the end of my rope and yell, which makes him cry, which makes me feel awful.*

Is there some secret to not losing one's patience in a situation like this?

A There sure is! The secret is to stop being so patient. It's your determination to help—no matter the cost—that's causing the problem. Frustration prevents effective learning. Therefore, once your son gets frustrated because your explanation doesn't immediately register, he's rendered himself incapable of understanding. From that point, the more you try to explain, the more frustrated he'll get, the less he'll understand, and the more difficult it will be for you to teach him anything.

At the first sign of frustration, you should do yourself and your son a favor by getting up and calmly saying, "When you get upset, it becomes impossible for me to teach and impossible for you to learn. Perhaps I'm not the right person to be explaining this to you, anyway. I think you need to save this until tomorrow, when you can ask your teacher to go over it with you again." Then, disregarding any protests, walk away.

That gives him a choice. He can regain his composure and politely ask you to explain it again, he can try muddling through it on his own, or he can wait until the morrow and ask his teacher, as you suggested.

If he calms down and asks you for yet another explanation, but then he gets upset again, separate yourself from the situation for the second and last time. Don't drag this ordeal out— twice is enough. After all, whether you can or can't successfully explain something to your son is not a test of your parenting ability. You aren't a teacher, and it isn't your job to make sure your child understands his lessons. That responsibility is shared by your son's teacher, whose job it is to communicate clearly, and your son, whose job it is to listen and ask appropriate questions. Parents who develop the daily habit of re-explaining their children's homework lessons aren't doing their children's teachers any favors. The child who learns to rely on his parents for this sort of thing isn't likely to pay adequate attention in class. Why should he?

This isn't to say that parents shouldn't ever provide help of this sort, because in most instances, when a child asks for an explanation, he or she should be given the benefit of the doubt. On the other hand, an effective consultant is the first to recognize when he's reached the limits of his expertise. He's the first to say, "I'm not the person you need for the job." That's not an admission of failure; it's an admission of fact. Furthermore, that admission doesn't diminish his credibility, it *increases* it.

So take a page from the effective consultant's rulebook and give yourself permission to *not* accept an assignment. In this case, your patience is *not* a virtue.

Q *Our son, Turner, is now in the third grade. Late last school year, after many problems involving homework, we started following your advice. Turner is responsible for his homework, and we are not. Turner is doing his homework, and we are not. Turner's grades and attitude toward school have improved. As you recommend, we are making him stop doing his homework at eight o'clock every evening, done or not. He's getting slowly better at managing his time, but he's recently discovered a way to beat the system. The clever little guy has started doing whatever homework he didn't finish the night before during our half-hour ride to school the next morning. I say we should not allow him to do this; my wife says, "Who cares?" I say the quality of his work suffers. My wife says, "Let him take the consequences." Whose side are you on?*

A Turner's. So you think he's learned how to beat the system, eh? Put that way, one is led to conclude that doing homework on the way to school in the morning is devious and manipulative and must be stopped. On the other hand, if we say that Turner's found a way to take *full advantage* of the system, then he rightfully deserves our admiration. He's ingenious, not devious, resourceful rather than manipulative.

The crucial link in all this is the teacher. In order for the plan to work, she must hold Turner to strict yet reasonable quality control standards. In other words, she must not accept work that is sloppy, unfinished, or clearly below his caliber. (She will undoubtedly be delighted to meet parents who actually want her to educate.) Under these circumstances, as sharp as he is, Turner will quickly see the folly of doing homework during the ride to school.

Q *The school my children attend expects parents to be involved in homework. It sends home regular suggestions on how we should discuss homework, help with assignments, and so on. Are you saying this is bad?*

A About the only thing such involvement accomplishes is better grades. At this point, you might ask, "So what's wrong with better grades?"

And I would answer, "Nothing, except that when parents are the reason for those better grades, the child in question is losing far more than he or she is gaining."

The most valuable learning takes place by trial and error. When someone is prevented from making errors, that same someone is also being prevented from learning. When parents become involved in homework, it is almost inevitable they will begin to take their children's grades personally. The more personally they take the grades, the more parents will act to prevent their children from making errors. Inadvertently, they short-circuit the learning process.

A child who is expected to do his or her homework in his or her own homework place may not always make A's and certainly will not always have error-free work. However, that child will learn more effectively from his or her mistakes. It has also been my consistent finding that even children who have been diagnosed with learning problems make better grades when they are guided toward doing their homework on their own.

Should parents ever get involved? Yes, it's reasonable for parents occasionally to answer questions, clarify directions, and even check papers. But limits must be set on parental help, lest the help become harmful. How parents manage homework sets a precedent that will have an impact on how the child responds to future challenges, including the challenge of successfully negotiating adulthood.

Q *Our eight-year-old son is reasonably intelligent and has no learning problems, but he takes forever to finish his work. An assignment that might take other children thirty minutes might take Ferdinand three hours. As a consequence of not finishing his work in class, he brings home a lot more work than his classmates, and then he spends nearly the rest of the day laboring over it at the dining room table. After observing him over several days, the school psychologist concluded that Ferdie's attention span is fine. He listens in class, participates well in discussions, and is by no means a behavior problem. The psychologist diagnosed Ferdie as a dawdler. He seems to go off into his own little world when there's work to be done, yet he recognizes he has a problem and tells us he wishes he could work faster. Is there something we can do at home to help him, or is this some aspect of his personality that may never change?*

A Who knows? It may well be that Ferdie is destined to be slow at just about everything he does, in which case he'll never make it as a jet fighter pilot. Then again, he may outgrow this problem as time goes on. One thing's certain: Nothing will be accomplished by getting upset about Ferdie's little quirk. In fact, the more upset you become, the worse the problem will get. Likewise, the more responsibility you accept for solving the problem, the less Ferdie will have to accept, and the longer it will be before his dawdling is cured, if ever. In that regard, resist the temptation to sit with him while he's laboring over his homework, coaxing and cajoling. If the problem is ever to be solved, it's essential that it belong to Ferdie. Some suggestions:

- Buy him an easy-to-use kitchen timer, preferably one that's digital so he won't have to contend with the ticking.
- Take an assignment and help him arrive at a reasonable estimate of how long it should take him to complete it. Initially, add ten to fifteen minutes to each of his estimates.
- Have him set the timer accordingly and try to complete the assignment before the buzzer goes off. If he succeeds, he earns a point. (Let him keep score.)
- Points can be exchanged whenever he likes for special privileges (having a friend over to spend the night) or things (a new toy). Before all this begins, help him come up with a menu of incentives and assign point values to each.

These steps will structure his cure, turn it into a game, and put the proverbial ball in Ferdie's court. Given his age (imagination peaks around age eight or nine) and the fact that he himself has expressed frustration over the problem, I bet Ferdie will enjoy this approach and rise quickly to the challenge. He can even play the game in class (and earn more points) using the classroom clock. Oh, and don't worry about him awarding himself points he really hasn't earned.

One last thing. When you're beginning to see some improvement, have Ferdie start doing his homework in his room. Homework done in a family area is likely to become a family affair, and there's nothing that robs a child of the truly lasting benefits of homework more than parents who are benevolently involved.

Q *My five-year-old has always been extremely inquisitive and seems to have an unquenchable thirst for knowledge. He started public school kindergarten this fall already knowing how to read and perform single-digit multiplication. (He's pretty much self-taught in both areas.) Because he has a late birthday, the school won't go ahead and put him in first grade, where he'd be eligible for gifted and talented programs. The problem is he's not being sufficiently challenged in kindergarten. His teacher agrees but tells me she doesn't have the time to write a special curriculum for him. What can I do?*

A If your son continues in a public school setting, this situation is likely to become more frustrating and counterproductive for all concerned. Instead of getting better, things could get worse, eventually resulting in a child who doesn't like school. I recommend you consider either private school or homeschooling. There's no point in my attempting to tell you how to correct this problem while leaving him where he is because it isn't going to happen.

In a perfect world, public schools would be able to individualize instruction for every student. In the real world, however, they are unable to be all things to all people.

As I recently heard a retired college professor put it, "Of course public schools aren't good enough. They never have been, and they never will be!"

Q *The private school our children attend places a great deal of emphasis on homework. We are concerned not with the homework itself but with the amount. It isn't unusual for our third grader to come home with three hours of homework a night, four nights a week. Do you think this is excessive?*

A One of the more unfortunate things achievement-test-score neurosis has spawned is an overemphasis on the value and importance of homework, and private schools pile on inappropriate amounts more than other schools.

Presumably, the thinking of many private school administrators is that learning and retention take place in direct proportion to the amount of time a child spends practicing a given lesson. There is some truth to this. However, studies show that when someone is learning a large amount of new information or a new skill, it's almost always best to distribute the total learning time into a number of separate, brief practice periods. See the discussion of distributive practice and massed practice on page 73–74.

The best research on human learning suggests that although homework is basically desirable, it should not demand much more than thirty minutes to an hour of an elementary-school child's time daily. With more time than that, returns are likely to diminish.

This makes good common sense when looked at from a practical standpoint as well. Six hours spent in school and one hour spent on homework amounts to a seven-hour academic day. That's enough to expect of an elementary-age child. Most high-school-age children should be able to tolerate two hours of homework, or an eight-hour academic day. The increase is also necessary to help prepare for college.

Q *My thirteen-year-old son waits until the last possible moment to begin doing his homework. He no longer has a set bedtime, but he must be in his bedroom after nine o'clock. It doesn't matter how much homework he has or even whether he has a test the next day; he doesn't crack a book until he's in his room. I've talked myself blue in the face about the importance of making good grades and told him that he simply can't be doing his best if he does homework when he's tired, but he says his grades are* *good enough (mostly B's with an occasional A) and that I should let him make this decision. This is driving me nuts! What can I do to get him to do his homework at a decent hour?*

A I agree with your son. He should be allowed to make this decision. I suggest that you do yourself a favor and abandon this issue forever. You're obviously causing yourself a lot of unnecessary aggravation and being a certified micromanager in the process.

You *have* to micromanage an infant or toddler, and you might be able to successfully micromanage a preschool or school-age child (nonetheless, I don't recommend it). But you cannot micromanage a teen without creating more problems than you solve. In fact, I'll go a step further and say that the attempt to micromanage a teen will solve absolutely no problems and is likely to create a slew of 'em.

Your obsessive concern about when your son does his homework falls into this perilous category. Do you really think he's going to get better grades if he does his homework when you want him to? I think it's more likely that if you force him to do his homework under your eagle-eyed supervision in the afternoon or early evening, he will rush through it, in which case his grades will drop—because you will have given him a good reason to prove you wrong.

Instead of trying to make your son do his homework when you think he should do it, give him permission to learn—the hard way if necessary—how to effectively manage his own time. Your job here is not to manage his time for him but to demonstrate that choices result in consequences. Good choices result in good consequences (better grades, more freedom), and bad choices result in consequences that are undesirable (bad grades, restrictions on his freedom).

For the time being, his grades are not a problem. But when he enters high school and academic demands increase, that may change, and you will have the opportunity to be the agent of reality. In the meantime, take a load off your shoulders and find a more constructive outlet for all that well-intentioned energy.

Q *Our seven-year-old son becomes very frustrated doing his homework almost every night. If he encounters a problem that gives him difficulty, he yells, pounds his fist on the kitchen table, and even cries. One of us will sit with him and try to calm him down and help him work through the problem. This usually works, but he might have four or five of these meltdowns a night. His teacher says he is smart and capable of doing the work; furthermore, she has never seen anything of this sort in class. He finishes most of his assignments on time without regular assistance from her. She sends homework for practice, meaning he's already had experience in class with assignments of the same sort. Also, he is generally not easily frustrated; rather, in other situations he's a fairly happy-go-lucky kid. What might be causing his frustration, and what can we do about it?*

A In this case, the context might be the cause. Before I elaborate on that cryptic remark, it would help to pin down the problem. What is it? Not his ability, according to his teacher. Nor his tolerance for frustration, since he does equally demanding work in class without meltdowns and generally finishes on time. His emotional eruptions are not par for the course with him. In fact, they only occur at the kitchen table, when he's doing homework. Hey, there we have it! The kitchen table causes his meltdowns.

You might think I'm kidding, but I'm not. The fact that he is allowed to do homework at the kitchen table places him in a situation where he can instantly receive your well-intentioned, albeit enabling, attention whenever he has a knee-jerk of frustration concerning homework. He encounters a bit of difficulty with an assignment, he plays the victim, and you immediately rescue him.

Get him out of there! He needs to be doing his homework in a private, personal area specially designated for homework, such as a desk in his room. Yes, I know most of his classmates' parents are hovering over them while they do their homework, but that simply means most of his classmates have parents who are making the same mistake you are.

Ask yourself: Does he do his work independently in class? The answer is obviously yes; therefore, he can do his homework independently. The kitchen has become a stage from which he can get attention by playing the victim. By the way, I'm not suggesting that your son's homework meltdowns are a means of manipulating or controlling you. That's psychobabble. I'm sure he's not sitting at the kitchen table plotting his next meltdown. It's simply a matter of Rosemond's Third Law of Parenting Physics: The more available the parent is to a young child, the more likely it is that the child will act helpless when frustrated. Conversely, the more distance there is between parent and child, the more likely it is the child will act competent when frustrated.

If your son doesn't already have one, put a desk in his room and stock it with everything he needs to do his homework. Tell him he can do his homework only at his desk and not to yell for you if he has a problem, because you won't come. If he needs help, he has to bring the problem to you. I'd go so far as to make a rule that he can receive your help only twice in any given evening. That will make him very selective when it comes to seeking your assistance. Worked with my kids.

Q *My eight-year-old daughter had an overall B average in third grade, but she has had difficulty completing assignments since the first grade. Mostly this is due to poor organization. The work may be completed but is often lost or forgotten. Her desks at home and school are a mess. We have made our expectations clear, given her responsibility for doing her own work, and* *have been holding her accountable. Still, she is struggling in school and at home. Furthermore, she says she is afraid to talk about problems at school because I will get angry.*

A Perhaps you are putting too much pressure on her. It seems that the most pressing issue, the one that must be resolved before she can move on, is that of her disorganized approach to her work. I can relate to this because before I could stop leaving things in hotel rooms (and usually losing them), I had to learn to keep my hotel room as neat as I do my home. I could not have solved this simply by concentrating more on not losing things. The cause— a messy hotel room—had to be dealt with first.

With that in mind, I recommend that you and her teacher work with her on her messy desks. Teach her how to organize her work. Provide her with supplies necessary to the goal (notebooks with file folder inserts, for example) and a good amount of supervision until she seems to get it. When you and the teacher feel you've done all you can to help her get better organized, begin using a Daily Report Card (Chapter 4) to monitor her organizing behavior. The report card can be as simple as a small index card with the date and the following statement: "At the end of the day, (your daughter's name) desk was neat, and she turned in all work due today." If the statement of achievement is true, the teacher signs the card. If not, she withholds her signature.

Your daughter brings the card home. If she did not earn the teacher's signature, she loses an important privilege. For example, she might have to go to bed an hour early. If she earned the teacher's signature, she retains her normal bedtime but is not rewarded.

It goes without saying that you cannot nag organization skills into your daughter. You're going to have to teach them, and teaching them will require that you be organized.

Q *My seven-year-old second grader would prefer to come home from school and play with his friend across the street. However, the rule in our home is that he must do his homework before he can play. Unfortunately, his friend can play after school, home-work or not. As a result, my son rushes through his homework and repeatedly asks whether he can tell his friend that he's almost done. I am not consistent about allowing that, which may be part of the problem. Sometimes, by the time my son has finished his homework, his friend has gone inside to start his, and the play-time opportunity has been missed. Needless to say, my son gets very upset. What is the best way to handle this situation?*

A The best way to handle this is to trust your son to get his home-work done. Stop enforcing this rule. Obviously, it's counter-productive, as are most attempts to micromanage. Your son is rushing through his homework, his mind is elsewhere, and he's regarding homework as a punishment of sorts. Simply tell him that you trust him to do his homework on his own but that he must have it finished by one-half hour before bedtime, at which point unfinished homework will be confiscated. If enforced dis-passionately, the deadline will help him learn how to manage his after-school time—perhaps more effectively than you are man-aging it for him.

Q *My daughter's second-grade teacher does not correct homework but only checks whether it was done. I find that my daughter often makes significant errors or leaves many questions unan-swered. When I ask why she didn't do the problem or assign-ment correctly the first time, she tells me it doesn't matter. How can I get her to take school seriously when the teacher doesn't?*

A I've heard this same story from numerous parents all over the country and have concluded that not checking the accuracy of homework or class assignments must be some newfangled education reform. You should most definitely discuss this with her teacher, but if you get nowhere, then you'll have to simply resign yourself to reality and begin pulling the slack.

When my children were in elementary school, I noticed that their teachers were taking a casual attitude toward the quality of their writing assignments. As you can imagine, good writing is important to me, so I simply informed the kids I would be checking their writing assignments at home and making them redo anything that didn't meet my standards. Their writing met my standards in no time.

I recommend you do the same. Check your daughter's homework and class work. When you find an assignment that isn't up to par, make your daughter correct it or do it over again. The reader may point out that what I'm recommending to this mother amounts to micromanagement, something I generally counsel against in any area of a child's life. That's true, but as we are told in Ecclesiastes (3:1), there's a time for everything. I am not recommending that this mom help her daughter with her homework or even sit with her while she does it. I predict that in no time at all, the quality of said daughter's work will improve dramatically, requiring less and less micromanagement on Mom's part.

Q *My son will be starting sixth grade at a new public charter school. This school uses a classical curriculum that does not draw from pop culture and sets high academic standards. The kids wear uniforms, are expected to demonstrate respect for one another, and are punished if they misbehave. My only concern is that they assign two to three hours of homework nightly. That seems excessive. Do you agree, or should I stop worrying?*

A It is heartening to know there are still schools out there that are not in thrall to regressive educational methods, schools that understand how to properly train a child's mind. The classical paradigm is language-focused rather than image-focused and stresses the relationships between subjects such as science and history. For more information, go to www.welltrainedmind.com. All education should fit this model.

To your question: I think that three hours of homework per night in the sixth grade is on the edge of being excessive. Two hours is not. The research strongly suggests that there is a point of diminishing returns where homework is concerned. At that point, learning becomes a negative experience for a child. On the other hand, that point varies from child to child. In the final analysis, the positives of this school experience far outweigh this one possible negative, so if I were you, I'd accept that an absolutely perfect academic experience cannot be found anywhere and stop agonizing.

4

Correcting School Performance and Classroom Behavior Problems (Without Drugs!)

More often than not, proper homework management is all it takes to turn around an underachieving child. But sometimes, it's not enough. Five out of ten underachieving children will begin turning themselves around—accepting responsibility for their classwork and homework—within four weeks of exposure to the ABCs. For the other five, nothing much will have changed.

Usually, the child who falls into that second category is suffering from Prolonged Lack of Initiative Disorder. He's become so thoroughly dependent on parental participation in his homework (and probably his life in general) that he's unable to muster what it would take to turn himself around, to accept responsibility for and solve his academic problems. If left to his own devices, he would probably choose to fail. Not because he *wants* to fail but because he simply doesn't know how to succeed. His parents, therefore, will have to take the bull by the horns and manage him toward making some correct decisions. I call it jump-starting the child's motivational motor. Although his parents will get actively involved in the design and delivery of a motivational plan, there are ways for them to do so without becoming responsible for his problems. An effective motivational plan must incorporate two key elements:

- First, the child's parents and teachers must agree on some means of monitoring the child's school performance. But all concerned must take the utmost care not to cross the line between monitoring and hovering. For example, the teacher should not sign a list of homework assignments the child prepares before leaving school and takes home to show his parents. Strategies of this nature are *compensatory* as opposed to corrective. They may temporarily shore up the child's performance, but in the long run they always, without exception, prevent the child from assuming complete responsibility for the problem. They are forms of hovering, micromanaging. As I've already said (but cannot stress enough), it is impossible to compensate for a problem and correct it at the same time.

- Second, the child must be made accountable (responsible) for the problem. In other words, the child—and only the child—must shoulder both the emotional and practical consequences of the problem. In specific terms, if the child fails to do his homework, no one should get upset but the child, and no one should be inconvenienced but the child.

Motivating Christopher

As an example of how these two elements—monitoring and assigning responsibility—can be creatively joined, take the case of Christopher, an eight-year-old third grader. Christopher was obviously capable but rarely finished an assignment in class. He spent most of the day "piddling," as his teacher put it: staring out the window, playing with his pencil, drawing, passing notes, and talking to other students. As a result, he carried both unfinished classwork and homework home with him. That is, he was *supposed* to bring his work home. In fact, Christopher would not have brought anything home had his teacher not made sure before he left school that he had a list of his assignments and the books and workbooks needed to do them.

Then, beginning shortly after supper, Christopher and his mother would engage in a world-class homework hassle until eight or nine o'clock every evening. She pushed, he pulled. She cared, he didn't. She went slowly crazy, he pretended not to notice.

Finally, Christopher's mother sought my advice. First, I had her implement my Homework ABCs. After several weeks, Christopher was as irresponsible and oblivious as ever. He was obviously in need of some creative management. With that in mind, I designed the Daily Report Card (DRC) shown here.

DAILY REPORT CARD

Student: Christopher Jones

Date:

Teacher's Instructions: Christopher is responsible for bringing this report to you at the end of the day. If all three parts of the "Statement of Achievement" are true, sign your name in the space provided. If one or more parts of the statement are false, put an "X" instead of your signature. Comments are optional but may be made in the space provided.

Statement of Achievement: Today, Christopher (1) completed his seatwork, (2) turned in his homework, and (3) everything was acceptable.

Signed
Mrs. Sally Smith

Teacher's Comments:

As the name implies, a Daily Report Card monitors a child's school performance on a daily basis. In addition to a clear set of instructions for the teacher, a means of rating behavior and performance, and a space for the teacher's comments, a DRC incorporates a Statement of Achievement—a concise definition of expectations.

Above all else, a Statement of Achievement should be attainable. It should reflect what the child is realistically capable of accomplishing, not necessarily what people *think* he is eventually capable of. A Statement of Achievement that is initially too difficult creates a no-win situation for the child. In that case, the program will fail, and the child's problems will get much worse instead of better. Later, once the child is performing consistently at the level initially defined, the ante can be increased by making the statement more difficult. Interestingly enough, I find that this is rarely necessary. Once a student gets on track with the program, his or her performance level almost always begins to exceed that defined by the Statement of Achievement.

Christopher was supplied with a folder full of DRCs, which he kept in his desk at school. At the end of the school day, he removed one from the folder and took it up to his teacher. If his performance for that day matched the goals set forth in his Statement of Achievement, she signed her name. If not, she put a large X in place of her signature. Note that it was an all-or-nothing proposition: The statement had to be completely true in order for Christopher to earn his teacher's signature. If even one part of it was false, she gave him an X.

The DRC provided the monitoring needed. The next component involved making Christopher accountable for his school performance. Up until this point, his mother had borne almost all the emotional and practical consequences of Christopher's underachievement. *She* made sure he did his homework. *She* made sure he studied for tests. *She* made sure his homework got back to school. And all of this doing-for-Christopher took a tremendous emotional toll on *her*. Meanwhile, Christopher was scot-free. No accountability for Christopher meant no change ever took place in his behavior. In effect, her best intentions aside, Christopher's mother had become an enabler. She was enabling his irresponsibility, making it worse instead of better. That needed to change, and change it did.

First, Christopher was now doing his own homework according to the ABC plan. Second, at the end of every school day, he took a DRC up to his teacher. She reviewed his work and filled out the report. He brought it home and immediately turned it over to his mother. If he had earned his teacher's signature, he was able to go outside, have a friend over, watch his normal allotment of television, and stay up until his normal eight-thirty bedtime. In other words, Christopher was able to enjoy his normal, everyday standard of living consisting of privileges, not rewards. However, if the DRC came home with an X instead of a signature, then Christopher's standard of living for the day was taken away. He was confined to the home, no friends could come over, he couldn't watch television, and he was put to bed at seven o'clock. If the report didn't come home at all, no excuses were accepted, and Christopher still lost all privileges. But he also had to go to his room after supper and stay there until his seven o'clock bedtime. This additional penalty for no report made it less likely that Christopher would conveniently lose those that were unflattering.

On days when Christopher earned his teacher's signature, a star was put in that day's box in the Star Chart shown below, which was attached to the refrigerator. If Christopher was absent from school for a legitimate reason (illness, vacation day), he earned a star automatically. At the end of the week, the total number of stars determined Christopher's privileges for Saturday and Sunday, as follows:

◆ Less than three stars: Christopher is on full restriction, meaning he cannot go outside, cannot have a friend over, cannot watch television, and goes to bed early.

◆ Three stars: In addition to the above, Christopher can stay up until his regular bedtime on Saturday and Sunday nights and can watch one hour of television each day.

- ◆ Four stars: In addition to the above, Christopher can go outside on Sunday and can watch two hours of television (his usual allotment) each weekend day.
- ◆ Five stars: Christopher can go outside on Saturday and can have a friend over on both days (even to spend the night).

This meant that on any given day of the week, Christopher was working not only for that day's privileges but for Saturday's and Sunday's as well. This combination of short- and longer-term incentives works much better than short-term incentives alone and is absolutely necessary for kids who attend after-school care and don't get home until nearly six o'clock, since most of their free time may already be gone.

CHRISTOPHER'S STAR CHART

Week begins: _____

MON	TUE	WED	THU	FRI	TOTAL

Note that it was Christopher's responsibility to remember to take the DRC to his teacher at the end of the day. It was not her responsibility to remember for him. And it was Christopher's responsibility to get the DRC home. If it didn't get there, no one went looking for it.

The teacher's job was simply to determine, at the end of every day, whether Christopher had or had not met the goals set forth in the Statement of Achievement. She took a few minutes to look over his work to make sure it was all there and that he'd done a reasonably good job with it. Then she made her mark.

All Christopher's parents had to do was enforce the rules. If Christopher came home without a signature, they didn't ask for an explanation. Nor did they get mad or give him a lecture. They simply kept him inside, kept him away from the television, and put him to bed early. They were calm, cool, and collected, and in so doing, they let the problem belong completely—in terms of both its practical and emotional consequences—to Christopher. Before, his mother was doing all the work. Now, he was doing his own work. Before, when he didn't perform up to par, his mother became upset. Now, when he didn't perform up to par, Christopher became upset. The monkey of the problem was thus transferred from Mom's back to Christopher's, and sure enough, Christopher learned to tame his monkey.

Christopher tested the system for two weeks. At first, he acted like he didn't care whether he received the teacher's signature or not. Then he tried arguing with his teacher when she gave him an X. When that didn't work, he begged, promising, "I'll do better tomorrow!" At home, he pleaded for just one more chance. When pleading didn't work, he cried and threatened to run away from home. He came home without the report a few times, saying that he left it at school, or lost it, or the school bully took it away, or it blew out the window of the bus, but always insisting, "I got a signature from my teacher! Really!" His parents listened, shrugged their shoulders, and said, "That's too bad, Christopher. We hope you manage to get your report home tomorrow."

When Christopher finally found out that the problem belonged to him and him alone and that no one was going to bail him out of whatever mess he made for himself, he began bringing home signatures. At first, he brought home just one or two a week. Then, slowly but surely, he began bringing home more and more until he was bringing home a signature nearly every day.

Once Christopher was on the right track, we kept the program going for another three months, just to make sure. Then his parents sat down with him and said, "Christopher, we're very proud of the progress you've made in school. You're doing the work assigned in class, doing your homework on your own, and your grades have gotten better and better. We've decided that if you don't want to carry the daily report any longer, you don't have to. But, if you decide not to carry it, we still expect good work in school. If you start having the same old problems, we'll have to start the reports again."

Christopher said, "I won't need 'em again." And he was right!

Civilizing Derek

Sometimes, a child's academic difficulties are simply a byproduct of classroom behavior problems. By resolving the behavior problems, you resolve the academic problems as well. As the following story about a second-grade boy named Derek illustrates, Daily Report Cards can be modified for this purpose.

Derek was your basic generic hellion. I met him and his parents the summer between his first- and second-grade years. They had been referred to me by the school counselor, who described him as the Great Pretender. In the company of adults, particularly if he was the center of attention, Derek was the perfect kid: considerate, mannerly, polite. Watching him work a crowd of adults, no one would have dreamed that Derek was the same kid about whom his first grade teacher had written,

> Derek seems to lack knowledge of how to relate to other children his age. When they don't give him his way, he hits, bites, and kicks other children and will then deny having done so even when observed in the act by an adult. Just the other day, he pummeled a child for accidentally bumping into him

*in line. A week ago, he punched a little girl in the stomach
and knocked the breath out of her. In the classroom, he talks
out of turn, shouts out the answers to questions without raising his hand, wanders around the room when he should be
working, and manages to distract and disrupt those around
him. Although he's smart and more than capable, he spends so
much time misbehaving that he ends up not finishing most of
the work he's supposed to do in class. One-on-one, however,
he's a charming little person.*

In other words, Derek was a budding sociopath. According to his
parents, he had been aggressive toward other children even as a toddler. He'd been an only child until age five, when a new brother came
into the family. The older the little brother became, the more jealousy
Derek displayed, and the more defiance, and the more disrespect.

His parents had all but given up on trying to get him to obey
even the simplest instructions. As his mother put it, "It's easier to do
it myself than go through the hassle of trying to get him to do anything." He tested limits constantly, and his parents had fallen into a
fairly consistent pattern of compromising and giving in to him in
order to maintain a fragile peace. Derek would do anything to be the
center of attention. He was a master of creating uproar. He started
the day by refusing to get out of bed and ended it by refusing to go
to bed. In between, he was demanding, disruptive, and disrespectful.

At the end of their second visit, his parents asked me why he
acted the way he did. I suppose they were looking for some high-
brow psychological analysis along the lines of, "Derek's expressions
of hostility are symptomatic of significant loss of self-esteem trace-
able to unresolved jealousies and feelings of parental betrayal related
to the birth of his male sibling, blah, blah, blah." Instead, I took a
deep breath and told them the truth: "I don't really know."

I let the shock sink in for a moment or two, then said, "I hate to
disappoint you folks, but if you want me to explain Derek's behavior,

I can't. I can speculate—and impressively so, I assure you—but explanations often tend to confound more than they clarify. For example, if we say that his problems stem from jealousy toward his brother, where do we go from there? Can you un-birth your second child? If jealousy is the problem, then it would seem logical to give Derek more attention. But we already know that the more attention he gets, the more he wants, and the worse his behavior becomes.

"This I do know: Derek is his own worst enemy. He dislikes himself for behaving the way he does, but hasn't the faintest notion of how to begin behaving better. That's where we come in. The adults in his life have to help him find his way out of the misbehavior labyrinth. And we will!"

Just before the start of the new school year, I held a conference with the guidance counselor and second-grade teacher. Upon review, we broke the overall problem down into the five most troublesome behaviors. They were (in no particular order):

+ Teasing other children
+ Physical aggression toward other children
+ Arguing with adults
+ Talking out of turn or during instruction
+ Getting out of his seat without permission

Those five behaviors—called target behaviors—were listed on an index card. Soon thereafter, the teacher and guidance counselor went over them with Derek, giving examples of each. The list was then taped to the wall behind the teacher's desk.

Every day, Derek brought the Daily Report Card shown below to school and, before the first bell, gave it to his teacher, who put it on her desk. Every time Derek displayed a target behavior, she called it to his attention, walked to her desk, crossed off the highest remaining block (beginning with block 6), and resumed whatever she was doing. Every target behavior resulted in the loss of the next highest block. If a target behavior or behaviors occurred on the playground or in the cafeteria, Derek's teacher crossed off a block (or blocks) when she returned to the classroom.

DAILY REPORT CARD

For: Derek

Date: _____

| | 6 | 5 | 4 | 3 | 2 | 1 |

Play Outside
Have a Friend Over
Watch Television
Your Normal Bedtime

Teacher: _____

Comments on back

When he came home, his mother took the DRC and attached it to the door of the refrigerator, which also had a home target behavior inventory that listed four misbehaviors:

- Teasing your younger brother
- Not doing what we tell you to do as soon as you are told, or not doing it properly
- Speaking disrespectfully to us
- Arguing with us

When Derek displayed a target behavior, the parent in charge said, for example, "You're arguing. That's one of your targets. You're losing a block." The parent then crossed off the next block on the DRC that was started in school. If that block was associated with a privilege, that privilege was lost for the rest of the day. On weekends and other nonschool days, a DRC went on the refrigerator first thing in the morning, and the parents administered it as described above. So with one DRC and two target behavior lists, we were able to include all of Derek's misbehavior.

The change in Derek was of the slow, fitful, two-steps-forward-one-step-back sort, but that's what everyone expected. It took a good six months before he was completely out of the proverbial woods, but he did it. At home, his parents eventually reported that not only was he more cooperative and respectful, but he was also playing patiently and gently with his little brother and even reading to him. At school, his behavior was equally improved. We suspended the program in March, informing Derek that he'd graduated but reserving the option of starting it back up again if his behavior began to deteriorate, which it never did.

High School Harry

For several reasons, it would be counterproductive to even attempt a daily report in a junior high or high school setting. First, because work isn't always assigned on a daily basis, teachers would often have no concrete means of assessing the student's performance. Second, if there was no free time during class—as is often the case in junior and senior high school—the rating would have to be obtained after the bell, which might make the student late for his next class and jeopardize his rating there. Third, junior high and high school teachers themselves have little or no time between classes, and ratings assigned under pressure are generally not accurate reflections of student achievement.

The solution is to use a weekly monitoring system whereby the student carries a report from teacher to teacher on Friday or the last day of the school week. The Weekly Report Card (WRC) I recommend for use with high school students is shown below. Note that the Statement of Achievement is cumulative, in that the teacher is being asked to rate how well the student has performed *to that point in the current grading period*. In other words, the first WRC of the grading period covers only the student's performance during that first week. However, the second WRC covers the student's performance during weeks one and two. Therefore, any deficiencies incurred during week one that are not corrected before the second Friday would also show up on the second report. The third weekly report would cover weeks one, two, and three, and so on.

WEEKLY REPORT CARD

Student's Name:

For Week Ending:

Instructions to Teachers: Student will bring this report to you on Friday of every week. Please take the time to respond to the "Statement of Achievement" by circling either YES or NO and signing your name in the space provided. **Please use ink. Note that both parts of the "Statement of Achievement" must be true in order for the student to earn a rating of YES for the week.** Comments are optional, but please feel free to use the space at the bottom for any you feel are appropriate. Thank you.

Statement of Achievement: Up until this point in the current grading period, _____ **(1)** is passing my class with a grade of "C" or better and **(2)** is not missing any assignments.

Subject	Teacher	Rating	Signature
Math	Adams	Yes No	_____
Lang. Arts	Smith	Yes No	_____
Soc. Studies	Jones	Yes No	_____
Health	Collins	Yes No	_____
Env. Science	Johnson	Yes No	_____
P.E.	King	Yes No	_____

Comments:

The fact that deficiencies follow the student in this cumulative manner means the student must resolve them in order to obtain satisfactory ratings. If the report was not cumulative, a student could conceivably get away with putting forth satisfactory effort on a selective basis, whereas a cumulative report requires consistently good performance throughout the grading period.

In the example above, the student is required to maintain a C average in every subject. The initial standard should be no higher than this, even if the student is capable of better grades. As the youngster becomes more responsible, the Statement of Achievement can be changed to reflect higher performance standards. Even if the student is capable of straight A's, however, the statement should never require more than a B in every subject. Nonacademic subjects such as band and physical education are optional and should be included in the report only if the child has been having difficulties in them or those teachers want to participate in the program. For that matter, the report can target only the subjects in which the youngster has had previous difficulty.

Also note that teachers are asked to use ink when filling out the report. This shouldn't require an explanation. I also recommend that parents obtain a sample signature from each teacher before the start-up of the system. Kids are smart, but teenagers are clever. If you don't get at least a step ahead of them and stay there, you'll find yourself reacting—after the fact—to one mischievously inventive maneuver after another.

Finally, the report is simple, which lessens the time it takes a teacher to fill it out. The more complex the report, the greater the chance that teachers will simply rubber stamp it from week to week. Before initiating a weekly report, the student's parents should meet with all the participating teachers as a group. This meeting can be arranged through either the guidance counselor or principal, and at least one, if not both of them, should attend. The importance of this preliminary step cannot be stressed enough. Remember that the report is simply a vehicle for communication. A face-to-face conference is the most effective way of getting everyone on board, setting the ball in motion, and preventing misunderstandings.

The preliminary conference sets the stage and puts everyone on the same wavelength. Everyone hears the same explanation and gets a chance to ask questions. The conference gives teachers a chance to have some input into such things as the design of the report, the actual wording of the Statement of Achievement, and when and how the student should present the report to them. It goes without saying that the more active their role in the planning process, the greater the chance of success for the program. Also, the parents' presence at the conference is a demonstration of their commitment to the goals of the program. It forms the basis for continued communication and creates a sense of teamwork that cannot be established as effectively through any other means.

Last, but not least, there's the matter of accountability. For a teacher to say, "Yes, I'll do this," in front of a group that includes several of his or her peers as well as a guidance counselor and the principal binds that teacher's participation in the program. The initial conference should not be dismissed without first scheduling a follow-up. This second meeting of the minds should take place midway through the grading period. (As I discuss later, it's generally best to begin a WRC program at the start of a new grading period.) This gives everyone enough time to develop a working feel for the program and identify problems that may require group discussion. The student's parents and each teacher should come prepared to make a progress report. However, the primary purpose of the second meeting is to make necessary adjustments in the design, logistics, or administration of the program. Future follow-up conferences should be held no less frequently than once per grading period, or more often if needed. An important topic to cover at the initial conference is the six rules of the program:

Rule 1: *The student is completely responsible for remembering to take a report to school every Friday (or the last day of the school week). This* simply means that parents are not to ask, "Did you remember to take your report?" before the youngster leaves for school on Friday. How the student wants to handle this is his or her business. It doesn't take long for most of them to figure out that the simplest way to avoid problems is to keep a supply of reports in their lockers at school or in their notebooks. Some students, after forgetting to bring a report from home, have improvised one at school. As long as the improvisation contains the necessary information in clear form, it's acceptable.

Rule 2: *The student is responsible for obtaining a rating and a signature from each of his or her teachers every Friday (or the last day of the school week).* The student must arrange with each teacher a convenient time to obtain this information. In other words, a teacher should not have to chase the student down after class on Friday if he or she has forgotten to obtain a rating. Although each teacher is going to have personal preferences concerning how this is accomplished, most will have the student present the report at the beginning of class on Friday, which gives them the flexibility of the entire period to complete it. Some teachers may prefer that the student return after school on Friday to obtain the rating. Students tend to complain that this inconveniences them with respect to after-school plans, to which I suggest the following reply: "No one is inconveniencing you. You have inconvenienced yourself through your own lack of responsibility. Put your priorities in order, and the inconvenience will end."

Rule 3: *The student is responsible for bringing the report home every Friday afternoon and showing it to his or her parents as soon as one of them arrives home.* No excuses are accepted if the student fails to either bring the report home or obtain a rating and signature from one or more teachers. Coming home with no report is equivalent to having a NO rating from every teacher. A rating without a signature, or a signature without a rating, counts as a NO rating. Unless permission has been obtained in advance, the student should come directly home from school on Friday, report in hand. "No excuses are accepted," it means exactly that. None. Zero. Zilch. The student can opt to ask the teacher or teachers to complete the report the next Monday, but they are under no obligation to do so. If they agree to this, however, and if the ratings are such that no restriction would have resulted, then privileges are reinstated for the remainder of the week, at which time another report is due.

Rule 4: *Under no circumstances can a substitute teacher sign the report.* If a teacher is absent on Friday, making it impossible for the student to obtain that teacher's rating, the student must obtain a note from either the counselor, principal, or assistant principal stating that the teacher was absent during the period in question. The note should be written in the Comments section of the report and must be signed in order to be valid. If a teacher is absent and the student obtains the required note, that teacher's rating is counted as a YES.

The first WRC system I designed was for a tenth grader whose grades had been in a steady state of decline for several years. The first Friday's report came in with three NO ratings, which meant the youngster was placed on complete restriction for the week (see Rule 5). The next report contained YES ratings from every teacher, but three of those ratings—and, coincidentally, the same three that had been NOs the previous week—were from substitute teachers. My nonsense detector went off like an air-raid siren. I called the school and discovered that, sure enough, there had been no substitute teachers. Realizing she hadn't done what she needed to turn the NOs to YESes, the student had sympathetic friends sign the names of three fictitious substitutes. Very clever, these modern teenagers. Ha! To tell the truth, at that age I would have tried the same thing under similar circumstances.

Rule 5: *The student's report can contain one NO rating without penalty.* However, if the student obtains a NO rating in the same subject two weeks in a row, he or she is on complete restriction (no special events, no television, no telephone calls made or received, no socializing with friends outside of school) until the rating in that subject becomes a YES.

Rule 6: *Two NO ratings in the same week result in full restriction until the next Friday.* At that time, if both NO ratings have become YES ratings, the student is no longer on restriction (unless he or she has incurred two new NO ratings). If one or both of the NO ratings remain unchanged, then Rule 5 applies.

As you can see, the consequences are quite simple. The student either retains (as opposed to earns) privileges or doesn't. Some parents and teachers have raised concerns about the built-in allowance involving one, and only one, NO rating. They ask, "Doesn't that mean that the student can get away with being lax in a different subject each week?" I answer, "Theoretically, that's possible, but it would take more energy to keep up with such a complex scheme than it would to just do the work required in each subject, and if a student's smart enough to figure it out, he's also smart enough to figure out what a waste of time it is."

Once the student's parents have held a joint conference with the necessary teachers, once the WRC has been designed and printed and the logistics have been worked out, the program is ready for lift-off. At this point, the student is informed of the plans that have been made on his or her behalf (don't expect expressions of appreciation), given a supply of reports, and told of the need to make plans with each teacher concerning how the report is to be handled every Friday. Encourage the student to make those plans before the first Friday of the program, but start the program on time regardless. If the student brings the report to a teacher who refuses to sign it, saying, "Sorry, but you should have made arrangements with me earlier in the week," it's the student's problem, as it should be.

Remember that the entire point of a program of this nature is to assign complete responsibility and accountability to the child for his or her school performance. The rules are designed to do just that. The child is responsible for arranging with each teacher a convenient time for obtaining the rating and signature. The child is responsible for remembering to take a report to school on Friday of every week. The child is responsible for remembering to take the report from teacher to teacher. The child is responsible for making sure each teacher uses ink. The child is responsible for obtaining the necessary note if there's a substitute. The child is responsible for bringing the card home. The teachers do no more than check their grade books once a week, give their ratings, and sign the report. The parents do no more than enforce the consequences of the program.

The program can be started any time; however, if the student is so far behind in certain subjects that he or she can't possibly obtain satisfactory ratings from those teachers, then the start of the program should coincide with the start of a new grading period. This effectively wipes the slate clean and gives the student a fair shot at success from the very beginning.

Typically, it takes a student about three weeks to get on track and begin bringing home consistently satisfactory reports. Once the student is bringing home good reports from one week to the next, parents should continue to run the program for an additional eight weeks, at the very least. This nails down the improvement and prevents a relapse. At that point, if everything is going well, then the program can be discontinued with the understanding that it will be reactivated if problems develop again.

Some people have asked, "What's the difference between this program and just putting the kid on restriction until the next report card comes in?"

The answer is that putting a child on long-term restriction is usually counterproductive. A child who can't see the proverbial light at the end of the tunnel is likely to just say, "Oh, what the heck!" and give up. As the next story illustrates, this isn't always the case; nonetheless, long-term restrictions (more than two weeks) should be used with caution.

A Few Words About Reality

Notice that rewards were not used to entice satisfactory performance out of Christopher and High School Harry. Why? Because rewards don't work to motivate those who aren't already well motivated, that's why. They may work for a while, but after an underachieving child has his fill of whatever reward is offered, the reward loses its motivational value. At that point, in order to renew the child's performance, the reward must be increased. That could go on forever.

The nature of a reward-based system means that the child is not accepting responsibility for the problem. His parents are accepting responsibility in the form of digging down into their pockets for the cash needed to keep the rewards coming. Meanwhile, instead of learning that good performance is its own reward, the child is learning that good performance is worth it only if there's something in it for him. He's learning to be stingy enough about good performance to keep the offers coming and to dish out just enough good performance to keep cashing in on them. I don't mean to say that children shouldn't be praised for their accomplishments, because they should be. But realize that praise doesn't create motivation; it simply helps maintain it.

A system that uses privileges instead of rewards is far more effective because it's reality-based. In other words, it's consistent with the way the world works. Let's say you begin misbehaving in your job: You start coming in late for work, you take too many breaks, and you're consistently behind schedule with the work you're supposed to do. Does your supervisor finally get fed up enough to say, "Okay, okay! I'll tell you what: If you'll do the job you're supposed to do this week, and do it well, I'll take you out and buy you a new car!"

Hardly. He is more likely to take you into his office and say, "I can no longer tolerate your misbehavior. As a result, I'm writing you up. If you continue to misbehave, I'll have no choice but to terminate you."

In other words, he threatens your standard of living. Everyone is motivated to protect and improve their standard of living. Once you become accustomed to a certain level, you don't want to lose it. In this regard, children are the same as everyone else. They are also motivated to protect and improve their standards of living. Adults measure their standards in terms of purchasing power; children measure theirs in terms of privilege: how often they can go outside, how far they can venture unsupervised, how often friends can come over, how much television they can watch, and how late they can stay up.

Threatening a child's standard of living is central to what I call the Agony Principle. It is a simple statement of accountability proposing that parents should never agonize over a child's behavior if the child is perfectly capable of agonizing over it himself. The actual consequence should always be an example of what I call the Godfather Principle. Borrowed from famous Sicilian philosopher Don Corleone, it states that in order to motivate someone to do what he or she is supposed to do, one must "make 'em an offer they can't refuse."

For comic relief, I make it sound sinister, but it's really not. It's simply the way the real world works. And if it's the job of big people to equip children with the skills they will need to successfully negotiate the real world, then it's our job to describe that world to them in accurate terms.

The Story of Eric: Part 1

As a further example of how the Agony and Godfather Principles work, take the true story of a fifth-grade boy named Eric. Eric Rosemond. Interesting coincidence, don't you think?

About a month into the school year, one of Eric's teachers called his parents and alerted them to the fact that Eric was, well, goofing off, although the teacher didn't put it quite that bluntly. "Eric's a great kid," she said, "And certainly capable of doing excellent work. But he prefers to socialize rather than use his time wisely. The problem is that he's already in danger of failing two or three subjects." The teacher suggested that Eric start writing his homework assignments in a notebook before leaving school.

"I'll make sure he's written his assignments down correctly," she said, "And you can follow up at home by checking to make sure he's done all his work."

Eric's parents didn't like that idea. "We appreciate your suggestion and agree that it would be a good idea for Eric to write down his assignments before leaving school," said Eric's father, "But to tell you the truth, his mother and I don't want to check behind him concerning his homework. We feel that Eric should accept that responsibility on his own."

After a pause, the teacher said, "But how is he going to learn unless we help him?" She sounded a bit defensive. Eric's father could tell that she was holding her irritation in check.

"We think he'll learn to be responsible once he discovers that the consequences of being irresponsible aren't worth it," Mr. Rosemond replied. "For example, we expect you to give him exactly the grades he earns. If you'll take care of consequences at school, we'll take care of consequences at home. What do you think?"

The teacher said she thought her idea was better but added, "He's your son."

That evening, his parents told Eric about the teacher's call. After recounting the discussion, Eric's father said, "We expect you to solve this problem, Eric. If you don't, then your mother and I will have no choice but to take a more active role in this matter. For the time being, however, your performance in school is your business, and we promise not to interfere."

Several weeks later, Eric brought home three D's on his report card. At least two of them were, in all likelihood, gifts from a teacher who couldn't bear to give F's to a child whose parents were so lax.

Eric's parents had a talk with him. They told him that although they didn't expect straight A's, they wouldn't—under any circumstances—accept D's or F's.

Eric's father said, "One of us will go to the school in four weeks and talk with your teacher. If she tells us that you have completely solved this problem, you will be allowed to leave the house. If not, you'll be confined another four weeks."

Eric's eyes grew wide and panicky, his lower jaw dropped open, and a look of complete incredulity spread over his face. "Wha-a-a-t???" he exclaimed.

"That's right, Eric," his father said. "For the next month, you'll be confined to the house after school and on weekends. You won't be allowed to have friends over or talk on the phone. After supper, you'll go to your room, where there will be no stereo, and remain there until bedtime. The good news is we promise that during the next four weeks we will not even ask if you have homework to do. The ball is completely in your court. Like I said, everything depends on that conference with the teacher four weeks from now."

"Well, uh, Dad," Eric asked, "Could you maybe go back to the school in two weeks instead of four?"

"Nope. Once every four weeks is already too often for us to be making trips to the school because of problems you should never have created in the first place. So that's the best offer you're going to get."

For the next month, Eric's parents followed through exactly as promised. During that time, they never once asked him if he had homework, never once checked to see whether he was doing home-work, never once called the teacher. They left him totally on his own, to be totally responsible for the problem and its solution.

When they went to see Eric's teacher, she gave them an excel-lent report. "I don't know what you did, but Eric's made a complete turn-around," she said. "He's turning in all of his homework, paying attention in class, and his test grades have been excellent."

"We didn't do much of anything," Eric's father said. "Just gave him a little time to think, and something to think about, that's all."

The Story of Eric: Part 2

Halfway through his sophomore year in high school, Eric turned sixteen and obtained his driver's license. No longer dependent on us or anyone else for transportation, he began spending less time at home, which is typical and perfectly understandable. However, it became apparent to us that he wasn't devoting sufficient time to his studies. When we expressed concern, he gave us the standard song and dance about high school being harder, to which we replied, "Yes, we know. And college is harder still, and the real world is harder than that, so it's time you started working harder, don't you agree?"

Then he said he didn't know if he could bring up his grade in one subject because that teacher didn't like him, to which we replied, "Kid, success in life consists of equal parts potential, perseverance, and personality. In other words, getting along with your teachers is every bit as important as knowing the subject matter. You need to straighten out whatever problems you've created in your relationship with that teacher, because that excuse simply doesn't fly around here."

Placed squarely in checkmate, Eric had no choice but to say, "I'll do better." But he didn't. A few weeks later, midterm reports came out and sure enough, his grades had slipped. "Don't worry," he said, "I'll bring them back up before the end of the grading period."

We believed him, but just to make sure, we borrowed a lesson from the Godfather and made Eric an offer he couldn't refuse. Every Friday, he was required to carry the WRC form discussed earlier from class to class and obtain from each of his academic teachers a statement of his current grade average in that subject, following the prescribed procedure.

We decided that Eric's grades had to average 85 or above, and no single grade could be below 77, which was the cut-off between C and D. If either criterion was not met, Eric would not be able to use the car until the next Friday, and then only if he had corrected the problem and brought home an acceptable weekly report. When I was sixteen, nothing was more important to me than being able to drive. I was confident that times hadn't changed.

The first week's report came in below 85, and Eric pleaded for us to give him one more chance. We said, "You have another chance next Friday. Meanwhile, you don't drive." That was the first and last week he failed to earn driving privileges.

We required the reports for about eight weeks, then we suspended them with the option of reinstatement if problems developed again. In the meantime, his grades came steadily back up to pre–driver's license levels.

The program made Eric responsible for his own freedom, so we weren't the bad guys. Furthermore, because he could see light at the end of the tunnel from one week to the next, the system was far more motivating than long-term restriction of the nebulous "until your grades improve" variety.

Thank you, Don Corleone.

Before We Go Any Further

Let's review what I've said thus far:

- First, the Homework ABCs set forth in Chapter 3, if implemented early enough, should prevent homework problems from ever developing.

- Second, five out of ten children with already-developed homework problems, after three or four week's exposure to the Homework ABCs, will begin turning around and accepting responsibility for their school performance.
- Third, of the other five children who don't show any improvement in response to the Homework ABCs, two or three will begin turning things around after being put on a motivational program. That still leaves two or three children. My experience tells me that those are kids who need special help of one sort or another, in addition to motivational management. In order to determine just what kind of help is needed, you'll have to gather and process some important information, and you may need professional assistance in doing so.

Evaluating Your Child's Abilities

Before deciding on a course of action for a child who doesn't respond to a motivational program of the sort described in this chapter, you must answer three basic questions:

- What achievement level is reasonable to expect of the child? In other words, what is the child's overall level of ability?
- Are the child's actual skills in reading, language arts, and math on a par with his or her ability level?
- Are the child's skills such that he or she is capable of doing grade-level work in school?

These important questions can often be answered by looking over previous report cards, examining the child's performance on standardized achievement tests, and talking with the child's teachers, past and present. This initial inquiry should render a good working picture of the child, and from that you can usually make a fairly accurate determination of the child's level of ability and his or her current level of academic proficiency and standing relative to grade level.

In some cases, this information is enough for you to begin making some strategic decisions, but if the initial investigation generates more questions than it answers, a more formal evaluation is called for. This is especially true if:

- The academic record is extremely inconsistent.
- The child's history has been complicated by developmental delays or chronic medical problems.
- The child has been having the same or similar academic problems for more than a year.
- The child began having problems almost from the first day of school.
- Academic performance is far below what everyone and the evidence says the child is capable of doing.
- Academic performance is below grade level.
- Grades or standardized test scores have deteriorated or fluctuated markedly from one year to the next.

If even one of these is true of your child, then you should obtain a formal assessment through a child or educational psychologist. That formal assessment will include, as its centerpiece, an evaluation of general aptitudes and abilities, accomplished with what is popularly known as an IQ test. At present, the most widely used of such tests is the Wechsler Intelligence Scale for Children–Revised (WISC-R). In addition, two or three tests of academic achievement will be given to determine the child's current achievement levels in reading (word recognition), reading comprehension, language arts (spelling and written expression), and math. In most cases, the psychologist will also assess the child's perceptual–motor functioning (eye–hand coordination).

It's important for parents to know that an IQ test does not determine how smart a child is. The concept of intelligence includes consideration of a person's creative abilities, social skills, emotional skills (e.g., social empathy, emotional self-control), athletic abilities, and even self-concept, none of which are evaluated by the WISC-R. It simply samples the child's abilities in only two areas of intelligence: verbal knowledge/reasoning and nonverbal reasoning. Both of these are highly correlated with school achievement.

By sampling the child's abilities, WISC-R answers the first of three important questions: What achievement level is reasonable to expect of the child? For example, a child who performs consistently within the average range on a test of general abilities shouldn't be expected to perform above grade level in school, and scores in the above average range tell us that the child is probably capable of a strong B average with minimal effort. Second, the child's performance profile can help in the detection and diagnosis of specific learning problems, such as learning disabilities and attention deficit disorder.

When I suggest that an evaluation of this sort is in order, some parents say, "We already know he can do the work."

"And how do you know?" I'll ask.

"Because whenever we sit down and go over the work with him, he shows us he can do it."

I hardly have the heart to tell these folks that they're comparing apples to watermelons and that the true measure of a child's ability level is not what he can produce when someone sits down one-on-one and coaxes answers out of him. The true measure is what the child can produce independently. Furthermore, I've yet to meet a parent who, in the absence of clear evidence to the contrary, didn't think his or her child was average or above in the intelligence department.

The second question—are the child's skills in reading, language arts, and math on a par with his or her ability level?—is answered by comparing the obtained measure of ability with the child's performance on the academic skill assessment. If there's a match—if the child's academic skills line up with his or her ability level and ability level is average to above—then the child's school performance problems are probably caused by a lack of motivation. However, if motivation of the sort described in Chapter 3 has been tried without success, then the problem may be related to emotional factors. If that possibility exists, the child's psychological condition should be assessed by a child psychologist or psychiatrist.

Are the child's skills such that he or she is capable of doing grade-level work in school? The third question is answered by comparing the child's scores on the academic achievement tests with what's expected of the average child in the same grade.

At this point, you should have enough of an information base to make some sound decisions. Those decisions—and remember, you've obtained an evaluation because a motivational program involving the sort of strategies described earlier hasn't worked—will involve either remediation or retention, the subjects of the next two chapters.

Questions?

Q *My daughter is having a personality conflict with one of her sixth-grade teachers. I don't know how it got started, but my daughter says this teacher has openly criticized her in class. No answer she gives when called upon is good enough. My daughter is not a saint, mind you. A perennial problem with talking in class has worsened during the last year or so. She's also entered a sassy stage in which she has to have the last word, no matter what. In other words, my daughter's capable of being a real pill. Nonetheless, I have reason to believe that this teacher isn't handling the situation properly. She's requested a conference with me, and I'd like your suggestions on how to approach her.*

A As long as the teacher is not being verbally abusive, and that's not likely, I'd recommend you support her. In general, when a child is having a conflict with an adult authority figure, I think it's best for parents to give the benefit of the doubt to the adult. It's important for children to see that adults support one another concerning disciplinary matters.

Once upon a time, if a child created a problem in school, the child's parents could be counted on to follow through at home. Adults supported one another's authority and, in the process, communicated a fairly uniform set of standards to children concerning their behavior and school performance. However, today's all-too-typical parent, upon hearing that the child was disciplined at school, is likely to challenge the teacher's judgment and defend or rationalize the child's actions. Not only does this permit children to divide and conquer, it also allows them to escape accountability for misbehavior.

Whenever either of our children came to us with a complaint about a teacher, our first question was, "Is the teacher treating every child the way she's treating you?" The answer was always, "No, she's only picking on me!" We'd respond, "Then you must be doing something to attract her attention to you, and the something must be inappropriate. We expect you to solve the problem, and quickly, or we will get together with your teacher and help you solve it." That usually was the last we heard of it.

There are very few teachers out there who do not have the best interests of children at heart. When a teacher says a child misbehaved, there's a 99 percent likelihood the child misbehaved. And although it always could be said the teacher could have handled the situation differently, the teacher probably handled it well.

This particular teacher may not be doing the best job of dealing with your daughter's behavior. But your daughter is capable of rubbing an adult the wrong way. At the conference,

I'd recommend you not only seek clarification of the problem but also voice your support and offer assistance. You just might find that aligning yourself with the teacher helps you as much as it does her.

Q *Our six-year-old daughter has developed a fear of going to school. Last year, with the exception of one or two teary mornings the first week, she went to school without difficulty. Likewise, the first day of this school year went well. The next day she balked on getting out of the car, and it's been downhill ever since. As soon as we get her up in the morning, she begins begging us not to make her go. Our reassurances make no difference. By the time we get to school, she's in a full-blown panic. It usually takes two adults to get her into the classroom. She clings, screams, and begs to be taken home. As soon as we leave, however, she quickly calms down. Her teacher tells us she's doing well academically and socially and seems in every other respect to be a normal first grader. We don't know what's causing her to be so afraid and don't know how to handle it. Can you give us some suggestions?*

A The origins of school phobia, as it's called, vary from situation to situation. In some cases, the child's fears are clearly related to problems at home. The parents' relationship may be conflict-ridden, a parent may have recently become depressed, or a sibling's behavior may be producing an overload of stress in the family. The child is afraid of what might happen at home in her absence. In these cases, she's also convinced that her presence in the home is necessary to prevent a family disaster of one sort or another. When family problems are precipitating the child's fears, the child's anxiety usually runs high throughout the school day, causing problems with both academic performance and social relations.

A child may also become school phobic because of fears that something awful is going to happen to her at school. Several years ago, for example, I consulted with the parents and teacher of a second-grade girl who, for no apparent reason, had suddenly started freaking out every school morning. It turned out she'd become upset at seeing the teacher reprimand another child and had convinced herself she would be the next target of the teacher's ire. All it took to solve the little girl's problem was an intimate, reassuring talk with the teacher.

Sometimes fears of this sort occur when a parent and child have not yet learned how to separate comfortably from one another. In other words, the child's anxieties are only one side of the coin. Unsticking parent and child from one another requires resolution of the parent's own need to be needed by the child. At other times, the child's fears defy explanation. They arise spontaneously, without apparent cause, and the more people talk to the child about them, the worse they get.

It goes without saying that if the cause can be clearly identified, it needs to be addressed. Given the history, your daughter's school phobia is probably one of the mystery cases and may forever remain so. I'd therefore recommend a loving yet assertive approach in which you first sit down with her and tell her she must go to school. Give her permission to fret and complain, but tell her she will go anyway. You'll continue driving her to school, but she's expected to go in by herself. If she balks, you'll walk her in, but that will mean she loses her privileges after school and goes to bed early. In so doing, you'll be making her responsible for the problem. That responsibility will motivate her to solve it. After all, she is the only person who can.

Q *I am a third-grade teacher who is dealing with several boys who have difficulty with self-control. Our school psychologist recommended an approach involving praise and rewards for* *good behavior. When I remarked that I didn't think you would endorse such an approach, she said your methods were negative and that punishment—because it causes resentment—eventually makes matters worse instead of better. I'd be interested in your reaction.*

A For more years than I will acknowledge, I've maintained that praise and rewards are generally counterproductive in dealing with inappropriate behavior. Praise works with children who don't really need it, I've said. Positive reinforcement of any sort, when used with a misbehaving child, will work for a short time. Then it will stop working. Additionally, the world does not work that way. When an adult misbehaves, he is not offered incentives to behave properly; rather, he is punished. The next question is obvious: Aren't adults obligated to teach children how the real world works (as opposed to how they might like it to work)?

Many psychologists and other helping professionals will counter that praise is an essential element of any behavior modification plan. At the heart of this conflict is the fundamental incompatibility of pragmatic and sentimental views of children and child management. Objectivity upholds the pragmatic view. A study reported in the *Journal of Abnormal Child Psychology* found that when praise was used in an attempt to modify the classroom behavior of children with serious problems, the children's behavior improved for a short time, followed by a dramatic decline to square one. On the other hand, when verbal reprimands were used exclusively (what some of my colleagues would call a negative approach), the children's behavior improved and remained improved. Furthermore, a combination of praise and reprimands didn't work any better than reprimands alone. The authors were careful to point out that whereas praising ill-behaved children when they behave well isn't productive, praise may have a generally positive effect on maintaining good teacher–student relations. Indeed, a parent or teacher cannot deliver effective discipline unless the child in question perceives him or her as a source of approval. Said another way, a child will not seek to please someone who acts as if he can't be pleased, and under those circumstances, the child is likely to resent that person.

A 2013 study found that teachers who are most like the stereotypical teacher of the 1950s—stern, demanding, critical when criticism was due, not interested in being liked by his or her students—obtained the best performance from their pupils.

So much for negative motivation causing resentment.

Q *My five-year-old daughter was so nervous on the first day of school that she threw up shortly after getting there. Since then, she's been crying every morning about having to ride the bus. She weeps on the way to the bus stop and while she's waiting, and I have to almost literally push her on it when it arrives. I admit I've given in and taken her several mornings. Every time, she promises me that if I'll take her just one more morning, she won't cry again. No such luck. When I ask what she's afraid of, she can't tell me, and her teacher says she's fine by the time she gets to school. A counselor friend of mine says my daughter's manipulating me. What do you think?*

A I think the idea that children manipulate their parents has been vastly overblown. The very concept implies a mental maturity that the typical five-year-old doesn't possess. No, a young school-age child who's crying every morning about riding the bus to school isn't trying to manipulate—as in conspiring against one's parents with aforethought—she's genuinely upset. Your daughter is really scared, but there are two kinds of really scared:

+ The child is really scared of an event that has happened or might well happen. Your daughter's fear would fall into this first category if, for example, the bus had been struck by an eighteen-wheeler and turned over the first morning she rode it. In this case, her fear would be reality-based, and you would need to take affirmative action of some sort. (Tangent: Do you know that the seat-belt law, especially as it pertains to children, can legally be ignored only by the government? I encourage my readers to put pressure on local schools to install seat belts, with shoulder harnesses, in school buses.)

♦ The child's fear is of something that has never happened and has a slim-to-none chance of ever happening, or it's a vague, undefined feeling of fear that the child can't put into words (i.e., "I'm just afraid!").

I'm reasonably certain your daughter's fear is the second type. She's obviously not afraid of school itself, or the teacher would be seeing a problem. If he hasn't already, the bus driver will probably tell you your daughter calms down by the time he reaches the next stop.

I'm sure you've said everything you can possibly say to your daughter about her fear. You've done what you can to help her solve the problem; now it's her turn. In fact, the only person who can solve it is your daughter. Believe me, an otherwise emotionally healthy five-year-old is completely capable of getting a fear of this sort under control. Tell your daughter that she has to ride the bus every morning. As usual, you'll walk her to the stop and wait with her if you have the time, but you will not drive her to school again, regardless of promises she might make. Assure her that it's all right to cry, that sometimes crying helps people get over fears of this sort. Don't promise her anything special if she doesn't cry, and don't make a big deal of it the first morning she's able to successfully suck it up. On that auspicious day, just tell her you're proud of her and let that be it. After all, getting on the bus without tears is no big deal. If your daughter sees firm resolve on your part concerning this matter, the fear will pass within a relatively short time.

Q *Four years ago, we adopted an eight-year-old girl with multiple developmental and behavior problems. Before joining our family, she had been abused and neglected and was in classes for educable mentally handicapped children. We've patiently but firmly taught her that behavior—good and bad—has consequences and that there is no excuse for misbehavior. We insist that she do her homework on her own and perform daily household chores. At this writing, she's not even close to being the same child. She's well behaved, she's responsible, and best of all, she made the honor roll at the end of sixth grade taking mostly regular classes! When she started seventh grade, she signed up for soccer with the understanding she had to maintain good grades, which she's done until recently. On her midterm report, several grades dropped to Cs with one D because of missing work. Her soccer team won the district playoffs and is slated to play in the state tournament. Should we let her play even though we made it clear at the start of the year that good grades and soccer went hand in hand?*

A Before I answer your question, I need to honor you with the "Tough-Love Isn't Always Warm and Fuzzy, But It's Authentic Love" award for not letting pity regarding the awful circumstances of your daughter's formative years cloud your parenting vision. Her behavioral and academic achievements are testament to your clear-headedness, your tenacity, your courage, and your most uncommon common sense. There are many, many parents of twelve-year-olds who have failed to accomplish in twelve years what you have helped your daughter accomplish in four. Your story is an example of super-responsible parenting, which every child deserves but which is increasingly rare. You are cultural heroes. Now, to the question of how to handle your daughter's academic slip.

As I understand it, the grades in question were on a midterm, or progress report. They are not final grades; therefore, she has time to correct the identified deficiencies. Furthermore, this downturn is not part of an ongoing series of ups and downs. In fact, it's your daughter's first step backward after four years of truly incredible progress. In consideration of all that, I'd definitely allow her to play in the state tournament.

You should sit down with her and ask what punishment she thinks is appropriate if her grades do not improve by the end of the term. My experience has been that a good kid—which she obviously is—will usually request a punishment that is completely out of proportion to the problem, as in, "I think you should keep me in my room the whole summer." In any case, cut the child's suggestion at least in half.

Q *I am a first-year teacher of four-year-olds in a private pre-kindergarten program. In my college program in child development, it was axiomatic that one always answers a child's questions, but I'm beginning to wonder. I have a child in my class who asks a constant stream of questions. He's intelligent and cute, plays very well with the other children, and has a wonderful imagination. Most of the answers to his questions are obvious. For example, I'll be cutting out an animal figure with scissors, and he'll ask, "What are you doing?" If I ask, "What am I doing?" he'll tell me. How should I deal with this?*

A The basic intent behind the idea that adults should always answer young children's questions—to promote intellectual curiosity—is a good one, but there are exceptions to every rule. Unfortunately, many child development programs treat this issue as if there should be no exceptions, ever, which is why you're beginning to get frustrated by this little fella's constant stream of queries.

You are not obligated to answer every one of this child's questions. You are obligated to respond, but your response can certainly be a firm but gentle refusal to answer. It's in this little boy's best interest for someone to help him discover that he can answer many of his questions for himself. As it stands, a question occurs to him, and he impulsively blurts it out. You can help him learn to control that impulse and begin thinking through many of the word problems that occur to him.

During a planned private moment, tell him he doesn't need to ask so many questions. He's smart, and he can answer many of them without your help if he just thinks a little while. Tell him that from now on, you're going to answer some but not all of his questions. On the others, you're going to help him answer for himself or simply remind him that he can answer for himself and leave it at that. I'd be sure to hold a conference with his parents beforehand, so they understand the philosophy behind what you'll be doing. It may be that they're experiencing a similar issue at home and would welcome your guidance.

For example, when your little interrogator asks what you're doing when the answer is as plain as day, you say, "Oh, you don't need me to answer that question," or "You can answer that without my help," or "That's the kind of question we talked about," or something along those lines.

You can also ask questions that help him discover the answers for himself. A number of years ago, in a similar situation involving a six-year-old girl, I recommended that her teacher give her ten tickets (rectangular pieces of laminated construction paper adorned with question marks) per day. If the girl wanted an answer to a question, she had to give up a ticket. When she ran out of tickets, the teacher couldn't answer any more questions. Within a week, this little girl, who everyone had thought was insecure and seeking attention, was asking fewer than five questions a day and looking much, much happier for it.

As they say, you can either give a man a fish or teach him how to fish; you can also give a child an answer or teach her how to think.

Q *Our twelve-year-old son is in danger of failing the sixth grade and, as usual, doesn't seem to care. Everyone agrees he's capable, just lazy. Worse, no punishment motivates him. We've grounded him, restricted participation in after-school activities (except scouts and church youth group), taken his television and video game system out of his room—nothing matters. At the moment, he barely has a life, but he's still doing nothing at school and is oblivious to his restrictions. Otherwise, he's a seemingly happy, mature kid. No one, in fact, can believe the problems we're having with him. What should we do now?*

A What you've described—an otherwise capable child who does next to nothing in school and for whom nothing makes a difference—is perhaps the single most frustrating, exasperating, maddening, and vexing of all parenting problems. In situations of this sort, which are not as uncommon as one might think, my first thought is the possibility of depression. Lack of motivation and disregard for consequences are possible markers of clinical depression. However, not all youngsters who fit that description are depressed, and depressed adolescents are rarely described as happy and mature.

If the problem isn't clinical (and I don't think it is), if this is just a case of colossal laziness, then you're doing all the right things. Whether restrictions motivate him or not, he should be restricted (although I approve of your exceptions for scouting and church youth group), and his room should definitely be barren. Whether he gets it or not, it's your responsibility to make clear to your son that sloth has a price: a lowered standard of living.

"But," you say, "it makes no difference to him!"

Right. Doing the right thing in response to a problem is no guarantee of improvement. For whatever reasons, some children seem immune to consequences of any kind. They just don't care what their parents or teachers do to them, whether it's positive or negative. These kids are usually passive, emotionally flat, and more interested (if the word even applies) in solitary than social pursuits. This combination of symptoms may look like depression, and sometimes it is, but more often, it isn't. It's just laziness, sloth, and so on.

Typically, this lack of drive becomes most pronounced in junior high school. My experience with children who fit this description leads me to conclude that the problem is usually not psychological. Someone who believes in fate might say these kids are destined to be underachievers. On the other hand, some of them turn completely around in high school, usually under the influence of relentlessly dedicated teachers.

So, as unproductive as it may seem, I recommend you stay your present course and resign yourselves to staying it for some time to come. And by all means, be as nonchalant about his restrictions as he is about his responsibilities. Making any sort of big deal about his grades is not going to make a positive difference, as you've already discovered, and probably will make matters worse.

Above all else, keep in mind that this is his life, not yours, and remember what Grandma said: You can lead a horse to water, but you can't make him drink.

Q *My second-grade son has received straight A's on both report cards this year. But he receives only satisfactory marks in effort. His teacher recently sent a progress report in which she says he often does not work to his potential. He fails to read all the directions on a worksheet and thus does not completely finish many assignments. This is compounded by the fact that he is usually in a hurry to finish his work, and therefore he's careless. The teacher says he's very capable. He reads well and with good comprehension. He can do math problems in his head, and so on.*

His teacher says his problems boil down to a need to stay better focused. As you generally advise, my son watches no television and has no video games. He has chores, has no problem occupying himself, and is well behaved. What can I do to make him slow down with his work and read all directions?

A This is a prime example of the enabling that often substitutes for a tough-minded approach to children in today's schools. Here's a teacher who instead of setting high expectations and enforcing them lets a capable child slide and then raises red flags because the child has figured out that he is being given permission to slide. The teacher is clearly saying that your son has sloppy work habits that result in incomplete assignments, yet she just as clearly does not penalize him. She gives him second chance after second chance to finish, correct his mistakes, and so on, and then gives him straight A's. Excuse me? Your son is not improving in his work habits because he is actually brilliant, a gifted child. Why, pray tell, should he change?

It's quite simple. A child who does not work to his potential should not be receiving A's. Saying that your son needs to be better focused is a way of hinting that he may have attention deficit disorder. Don't go there!

This problem does not reside in your son's nervous system; he focuses quite well when he must. Rather, it is a function of this teacher's well-intentioned but dysfunctional approach. Confront her firmly but politely and inform her that you cannot motivate your son to be more conscientious as long as she gives him A's for substandard work. She needs to penalize him for turning in assignments that are sloppy or incomplete. Furthermore, his grades should reflect his first attempt at an assignment, not his second or third. Tell her you are willing to follow through with penalties at home for grades that are below par, but you cannot justify penalizing him for making the highest grades possible.

This is not education; it's coddling. And coddling does not bring out the best in a child. Rather, as this example shows, it brings out the worst.

Q *At least twice a week, my son's first-grade teacher sends home assignments he should have finished in class but didn't, because of dawdling. It's obvious the teacher doesn't, and won't, penalize him for this. I feel we should penalize him at home. Do you agree?*

A Yes, I agree. Obviously, lack of ability is not the problem. You have an opportunity here to nip in the bud a problem that will, if left unchecked, only get worse over time. I recommend making it a rule that if he brings unfinished work home one day of the school week, he'll be restricted one weekend day, confined to the house with no television and no visitors. If he brings unfinished work home two or more days through the week, he'll be restricted through the entire weekend. That should constitute an offer he can't refuse, but because he's a child, he will refuse it, at least until he becomes convinced you are serious.

Q *Our son's new first-grade teacher gives children smiley faces for behaving properly. At the end of the week, they trade them in for prizes. On the other hand, nothing of any real consequence happens when a child misbehaves. At home, when our son misbehaves, we punish him. We are concerned that the difference between our approach and the teacher's may cause our son confusion. Also, doesn't giving rewards for good behavior teach that proper behavior is deserving of something special?*

A Indeed, children should be taught that responsible people do the right thing simply because it is the right thing to do, not because it will result in rewards. Behavior modification strategies of this sort (the method the teacher is using is known in psychological circles as a token economy system) undermine that understanding.

Researchers have found that reward-based motivational and management systems seem to work best with children who are already well behaved and would continue to be well behaved without reward. Studies have also shown that the most well-behaved, well-adjusted children tend to come from homes where parents punish misbehavior. As regards children with behavior problems, rewards seem to have no lasting positive effect and may even be counterproductive. My own experience, both as a clinician and a parent, confirms these findings. Despite the evidence, however, most school systems persist in dispensing rewards.

The sad fact is that a good number of parents will not support the use of punitive discipline by their children's teachers, much less even acknowledge that their children are capable of wrongdoing. When their children are punished at school, these parents complain vociferously. Some even threaten legal action.

As a consequence, many schools both private and public tend to take the low road where discipline is concerned, avoiding punishment at all cost. Unfortunately, this compromise almost surely results in more children being referred to outside professionals and winding up on behavior-controlling medication. The solution is for parents to support the use of effective punitive discipline methods at their children's schools. Most important, parents need to support the use of punishment with their own children, as opposed to only supporting it for other people's children.

But let me assure you that your son is in no danger here. The discipline used by his teacher is not going to cause him the slightest confusion, nor will it lessen the effectiveness of your discipline at home. As should all parents, ask your son's teacher to let you know if and when he misbehaves in class and follow through by punishing him at home.

In the final analysis, a teacher's discipline, no matter how effective, is not as powerful a deterrent as effective discipline delivered by a parent. I've said it before, but it's worth repeating: A child who misbehaves in school and suffers no consequence at home will continue misbehaving at school, no matter how effective a teacher's discipline.

Q *Our eighth-grade son is obviously intelligent and is in his school's gifted and talented program. Furthermore, he scored in the top 5 percent on his last national achievement test. But his grades have been consistently average and have recently gone from bad to worse. The problem is not only his grades but also his attitude at home. He refuses to discuss his school problems with us and is often defiant and disrespectful, especially when we try to talk to him about our concerns. His favorite pastime is his video game console, which he probably plays to excess. We don't have these problems with our other children and are at a loss as to how to motivate him. Suggestions?*

A Your son needs a major wake-up call, but he's not alone in that regard. Underachievement is epidemic among today's youth. Factors involved in this torpor include a sense of entitlement (which they have come by honestly), grade inflation, parent overinvolvement in homework, and electronic diversions. It is significant that nearly every time I hear of a boy who is performing well below his ability level, I also hear that he is spending a disproportionate amount of time playing video or online games. For girls, the equivalent seems to be texting.

My first suggestion, therefore, is that you make the video game console disappear, permanently. After I wrote a newspaper column on a seventeen-year-old boy who was obsessed with playing online games, I received several letters from counselors and addiction specialists thanking me for pointing out what they have known for some time: Video games are addictive, literally. The problem is that unlike a drug problem, this addiction is legal. As one counselor pointed out, "Parents seem to think that as long as their children are at home and safe, then they are okay. They don't seem to notice the subtle declines in creativity, affect, motivation, and simple thought processes (associated with video game addiction)."

Take that nefarious device and toss it in a trash bin that's at least five miles from your house. When your son comes home and wants to know where it's gone, say, "Your priorities are obviously out of whack, and it's obvious that you don't realize they're out of whack, so we have taken the first step toward helping you get them into whack."

He may become extremely angry, irrational, and even threatening. That's how addicts behave when they are suddenly cut off from their "jones." In that case, you need to keep your cool and say as little as possible. If he gets you to defend your decision, you'll find yourself embroiled in an escalating, nonproductive argument of the worst sort. Make clear that there will be no negotiation or discussion—that you've done what you've done and that's the end of it. Then stand back a respectful distance and let his emotions run their course.

When he's calmed down enough to listen to you (which may take a few days, a week, or even two), point out that he has never taken seriously his academic responsibilities. You took his video game away because it was siphoning his motivation and sense of decorum, and you are prepared to go even further. In that regard, remind him that in two years, he will be eligible for a driver's license, and then say something along these lines: "Driving involves responsibility for other people's lives, which is the biggest responsibility of all. The fact that you don't work up to your ability in school doesn't threaten anyone's life, so it's not as big a responsibility as driving a car. The way we see it, if you won't deal properly with your school responsibilities, then we won't be able to let you get behind the wheel of a car. For that to happen, your grades need to reflect your ability, and although you don't often act like it, you are a person of significant ability."

It's time for your son to be confronted with Real World Principle Number One: If you don't do what you're supposed to do, you don't get to do what you want to do. Come to think of it, that's Real World Principles Two and Three as well.

Q *Our son's fifth-grade teacher has recently sent home notes to the effect that our little darling isn't paying attention and is missing homework assignments. When I asked what in-school consequences he receives, I was told that he receives none unless I specifically so request. In other words, unless teachers inform parents of problems (which doesn't reliably happen), the problems go unpunished. When I hear of a problem, I take away privileges for a week or more, and my son knows that if he brings home a report card with a bad grade or behavior report, privileges are removed for the next grading period. Is this appropriate, and what can I do to get the school to do their part?*

A To your first question, yes, what you're doing in response to being notified of problems at school is appropriate. You're my kind of parent—all the more so because you have the courage to hold your son accountable in a culture of excuses.

To your second question about getting the teacher to do her part, the answer is probably "nothing." In all too many of America's public schools, classroom discipline is a farce. It's not that teachers don't want to discipline; it's that they are specifically prohibited from doing anything effective when a child misbehaves academically or socially.

The problem (and this shouldn't surprise anyone) is lawyers and the law. For one thing, a school can be sued if a child is punished for behavior that is later discovered to be symptomatic of a disorder with which the child is supposedly afflicted. So if Johnny is punished in November for exposing himself to the class at recess, and the next March a psychologist determines Johnny has childhood bipolar disorder, Johnny's parents can sue school officials for victimizing Johnny. I know that sounds completely unbelievable, but it's the honest-to-Josephus truth.

As a consequence of institutionalized insanity of that sort, one of a principal's primary responsibilities is to keep the lawyers at bay. So, playing it safe, more and more of America's public schools are discipline-free zones. Another aspect of the problem is that teachers report problems at great risk to themselves. Fifty years ago, parents were unequivocal in their support of teacher authority. All too many of today's parents, when they are informed of a problem, rise to their children's defense. Sadly, all too many of today's principals, when parents get upset, will not back their teachers. Needless to say, children are no dummies. Even the child with a serious learning disability is quick to figure out that a school's discipline policy is a sham and that his parents are desperate to believe that he is incapable of dirty deeds.

As your son's teacher told you, you can specifically empower the school to punish him for not turning in assignments, not paying attention in class, and so on, but that raises the question: What, in the school's view, constitutes punishment? Even with your permission, the teacher may not be permitted to do anything more draconian than depriving your son of a smiley face sticker at the end of the day.

In short, this is probably a losing battle on your part. Just do your duty at home.

Q *Our seventeen-year-old is a perennial underachiever. He's had up and down grades all through school. Other than that one problem, he's a great kid—respectful, sensitive, helpful,* *reasonably well behaved. With graduation in a little over a year, we're starting to worry that he may not make it in the real world. We've tried using every carrot and stick we could think of, but nothing has worked. He is currently making four F's. Our current tack is to do nothing but simply tell him that the consequences of underachievement as an adult are going to be far worse than ours. Are we on the right track?*

A It seems to me that you're on no track at all—this train is de-railed. He seems to have no appreciation of the fact that Real Life is not going to put food on his plate. Talking yourselves blue in the face is not going to correct his myopia.

I'd tell him that the responsibility of doing his best in school is minor compared to the responsibilities involved in driving a car. For example, underachievement puts no one else's life at risk, but driving a car does. Since he can't deal with the lesser respon-sibility, you can no longer trust him with the greater responsibil-ity. You'll let him drive again when his grades come up to par.

I'd also take the door off his room: "You need to get used to being homeless, because that's a distinct possibility in your life. Homeless people have no privacy, so neither will you until your grades come up."

If experience serves me well, those two moves will put him in checkmate, and he will slowly begin doing what's necessary.

Q *We have discovered that our seventeen-year-old son recently went to school, checked in, and then left a short time later. To our knowledge, he's never done this before. His explanation was that he was bored and just wanted to have some free time. We are at a loss as to how to respond. What consequence or con-sequences do you think are appropriate?*

A This is a great question because it raises some very important considerations about the use of consequences.

Today's parents seem to believe two things about consequences: First, when a child misbehaves, the parents should apply a negative consequence; second, properly selected and properly used consequences do work. There is some truth to both of these assumptions, but both come with caveats.

To the first assumption: Consequences should be used very conservatively. When they are used liberally, the parents in question are guilty of trying to micromanage misbehavior. Any type of micromanagement will result, ultimately, in negative outcomes. For example, overusing consequences can lead to full-scale rebellion.

In order for me to answer your question with any degree of confidence, I would need some background information. Is your son a repeat offender? Does he have a history of willfully irresponsible, rebellious behavior? Are his grades up to his ability level? In other words, is this a blip, or is it part of an overall pattern that has been developing over some time? If it's a blip, then the fact that he was caught is price enough. If it's part of an overall pattern, then it's definitely time to apply consequences.

You could take away all electronic devices—computer, cell phone, video game, MP3 player—until certain behavior and academic goals have been met and the improvement has sustained itself over, say, a month. But that would not be my response if he's a generally good kid who just took a brief walk on the wild side one day. My response to that would be, "I hope, for your sake, this doesn't happen again."

To the second assumption: Consequences work reliably and predictably, with dogs, rats, and other lower life forms. They do not work reliably with human beings. It may surprise the reader to learn that no research psychologist, including B. F. Skinner (the father of behavior modification theory), has ever conclusively demonstrated that rewards and punishments have predictable outcomes when used on humans. In fact, there is a growing body of anecdotal and research-based evidence to the effect that rewards can actually lower performance and stimulate an increase in misbehavior and that punishment can similarly backfire. Those risks increase the more rewards and punishments are used.

When you hear a parent say, "I've punished my child consistently for misbehaving, and he keeps right on misbehaving," the problem may be the first half of the parent's statement.

Q *Our son started full-day kindergarten in September. For the first three months he had no problem with his behavior at school, but for the past few weeks he has gotten in trouble for talking and not listening, and he spit at a child at school today. Taking away privileges hasn't made a difference in his behavior. He was always such a well-behaved child so we are at our wits' end as far as what to do. Any suggestions for punishment would be greatly appreciated.*

A Sometimes punishment is the answer for a classroom behavior problem; sometimes it isn't. In this case, I am reluctant to recommend punishment because your son's problems began suddenly after three initial months of good behavior. That's certainly puzzling. It suggests that something happened—and is still happening—at school to cause this sea change in your son's attitude. That intuition is strengthened by the fact that he's never been a discipline problem.

Is the teacher young or inexperienced? Did some incident occur—perhaps an embarrassing one—in class or on the playground that might have caused the other children to change their attitude toward your son? Is he being teased by his classmates? Did his best classroom friend suddenly decide to abandon him in favor of some other child? You first need to do a certain amount of detective work in order to determine whether such an incident did occur. The fact that taking privileges away hasn't set your son back on the right path leads me to think there's more going on here than meets the eye.

Sometimes a seemingly small event can rapidly cascade into a major problem. If so, then it may be that things have gone downhill to the point where a change of teacher, even a change of school, is called for—a fresh start, in other words.

If these questions don't uncover any specific problem, it may be that a classroom behavior problem is just that and nothing more. I generally recommend a consequence-based approach involving loss of privileges on bad school days. This requires that the teacher provide daily feedback concerning the child's behavior. For example, she can e-mail a brief daily report to the parents at the end of every school day.

At-home privileges depend on a good report, and the best results are obtained when the daily report involves no shades of gray. In other words, the child was either incident-free or not—and exactly what constitutes an incident must be defined clearly in advance. One such event results in the child losing all privileges including television, all other electronic entertainment, and after-school activities. In addition, his bedtime is moved forward at least one hour. Two bad days during the school week result in loss of privileges on the weekend.

The combination of daily and weekend consequences usually proves to be enough of a persuader. Sometimes, improvement is seen almost immediately; sometimes, it takes a few weeks. The secret, as always when the issue is discipline, is consistency on the part of both parent and teacher.

Q *My six-year-old daughter is in the first grade, and other than the papers she brings home, I have no idea what or how she's doing. I realize it's not my job to keep tabs on every minute of* *her education, but I feel completely out of the loop. Why? She won't tell me! I ask her every day what she's doing in class, but I never get an answer other than "I don't remember" or "Nothing." The teacher sends home general information, but I get no specifics from my daughter. She's been tested and falls into the gifted category; therefore, it's important to me that she be challenged in class and learn something significant during the year. The first lesson I'd like her to learn is that when Mom asks what's going on in class, she must give me a decent answer. Do you have any suggestions on how I can get her to open up to me?*

A   My suggestion is founded on the fact that nature abhors a vacuum. You've already discovered that badgering your daughter for information yields nothing but passive resistance. As it stands, you have become a slave to your anxieties, all of which are probably unfounded, and you are beating your head against the proverbial brick wall. Create a vacuum. Stop asking, and your daughter will eventually open up. Probably. And if she doesn't, well, the teacher will certainly let you know if something is amiss. No news from school is almost always good news!

My experience leads me to believe that a child who doesn't open up to parents about school is a child who either wants to hide something or wants nothing more than to own her school experience and is resisting well-intentioned attempts at micromanagement on the part of her parents. I have to believe your daughter falls into the latter category. If you agree, then I strongly advise you to count your lucky stars, relax, and back off. Stop asking so much as "How was your day?" Let her tell you, which she will, if she feels like doing so. The more you pressure her to talk, the more she will resist, simply because you are giving her something to resist against, an opportunity no child can resist.

To the matter of her being gifted, there is no evidence that a highly intelligent child needs an ideal school environment in order to put her talents to good use. Nor is there evidence that the best possible school environment is guaranteed to produce a child who does well in life. The most successful people are self-directed, not necessarily brilliant. Your daughter is obviously self-directed. Conclusion: She does not need much direction.

Q *According to his kindergarten PE teacher, our son has recently started refusing to participate in class. He sits off to the side and pouts. She said he won't tell her what the problem is. This is a very active child who comes home and plays outside with other kids most of the afternoon. We tried to talk to him about it, but like the teacher, we got nowhere. What should we do?*

A If your son has no difficulty making friends and enjoys being active, then the first thing to do is play Sherlock Holmes and look for clues that might explain this mystery. Start your sleuthing by talking to the PE teacher. Maybe something happened in class recently that might have caused your son embarrassment. If that conversation doesn't help clear up the mystery, then call other mothers and ask if they've heard any comments about PE from their kids. Have their children said anything about your son and his refusal to participate? If there's a way you can observe the class without your son knowing, I'd consider doing that as well. Hopefully, you'll discover the problem and be able to do something to solve it. He may have misinterpreted something that happened in class one day, for example, and doesn't have the language skills to put it into words.

If you come up empty-handed, then the explanation may be that there is no explanation. As also happens with adults, children sometimes get into funky moods for no good reason. Like dark clouds passing in front of the sun, these moods hang around for a while then leave as quickly as they showed up. Most people have experienced spontaneous lows like this at times and not been able to make sense of and explain the feeling. You wake up one morning and just don't feel like going to work, but you can't identify any specific incident that might have caused you to feel that way. Regardless, you get up and go, but you feel under the weather for several days.

Occasional, short-lived moods of that sort are normal. After all, life has its ups and downs, and our internal lives have rhythms too. Blue funks of that sort become problematic only when they increase in frequency and duration and begin to interfere with a person's ability to carry out day-to-day responsibilities. Something along these lines may be what's going on with your son. If so, that would explain why he is having difficulty putting his feelings into words.

If you reach the conclusion that there's nothing problematic about PE, then it's important that your son participate. I think the application of some gentle but irresistible pressure will be enough to persuade him to do so. Tell him that not wanting to participate in PE means he must not be getting enough sleep. In that event, he can't play outside after school and has to go to bed early every evening until the next PE class. Meanwhile, the teacher should not make a big deal of his pouting. She should simply assign him to a chair off to the side of the activity and not pay any attention to him.

I have a feeling that this is just one of those stumbling blocks that occasionally crop up in the course of raising a child (or, for the child, are just part of growing up) and that everyone will move past it fairly quickly.

Q *My eleven-year-old son cuts corners on everything. If he does a chore, he'll leave the cleaning products behind. If his bed is hard to make, he hides the sheet in the closet and throws the blanket over the bed. Concerning his schoolwork, he doesn't bother studying for tests (figuring he gets A's anyway). We're now* *seeing this in his soccer practices, where he's started literally cutting corners. How can we get a handle on this bad habit?*

A Because it's not blatant, as in blatant disrespect or disobedience, this sort of problem can be difficult to get a handle on. Today's parents believe in parenting technology—that for every behavior problem, there's a solution. The fact is that parents cannot solve all the possible problems a child may develop. They can't solve any of those problems, in fact. It doesn't matter what the problem is, parents can only put pressure, in the form of consequences of one sort or another, on a child in hope that the pressure will motivate the child to solve it. Some children give in to the pressure, some don't. Sometimes, a child doesn't solve a problem until he's in a state of crisis because of it, and the crisis in question may not occur until he's well into adulthood.

When parents use consequences in the mistaken belief that there is a magic consequence that will solve the problem in question, they miss the point and are possibly setting themselves up to fail. The purpose of consequences is simply to demonstrate that in the real world, bad behavior causes bad things to happen, sooner or later. Hopefully, the child will get it and solve the problem.

If the child doesn't solve the problem, that doesn't necessarily mean the consequence was not the right one to use. That belief often causes parents to try one consequence after another in a chaotic attempt to find the one that will turn the proverbial wheel. Perhaps the consequence in question was insufficient—it didn't apply enough pressure. On the other hand, it may be that the consequence was sufficient, but the child wasn't ready.

Having delivered the necessary disclaimer, my recommendation is that you focus on one problem area and one only. Don't bite off more than you can chew by attempting to solve the chore, school, and soccer problems in one fell swoop. Start with chores. Make a list of the specific things he does to cut corners where chores are concerned. Suspend a privilege or package of privileges until he's solved the "cutting corners when he does chores" problem and has had no relapses for a month. Mind you, his rehabilitation may take four weeks; then again, it may take four months or four years. Be ready to hang in there and continue imposing the consequences until he gets it. And be ready to accept that you are not the appointed agents of change concerning this problem. The appointed agent of change may not enter his life until he's forty-five years old. We've all seen that happen, haven't we?

Here's what I call the Hang in There Principle: If a child does wrong things and the child's parents do right things and the child keeps on doing wrong things, then the child's parents should simply keep on doing the right things.

CHAPTER

5

When to Remediate

Remediation consists of providing a child with academic instruction over and above what he or she is receiving in a regular classroom setting for the purpose of correcting academic deficiencies. It includes in-school remediation delivered through a school's special education department, private individual tutoring, and group tutoring of the sort that is usually obtained through a learning center.

Excluding situations where a child's parents simply want the child's classroom education to be supplemented by outside instruction, remediation is called for if:

- The child's academic skills test significantly below ability level in one or more areas.
- The child's ability level is average or above, but certain academic skills are below grade level.
- A significant discrepancy exists between the child's achievement levels in reading, language arts, spelling, and math.

Keep in mind that it's entirely possible and not unusual for a child to test at or even above grade level but below his or her ability level. Therefore, the mere fact that a child's academic skills are commensurate with grade-level expectations does not rule out the advisability of remediation.

A significant discrepancy between achievement and ability might result from a learning disability, emotional factors, a motivation deficit, excessive use of electronics, or a general indifference toward education on the part of the child's parents. It might also mean that the child got off to a bad start in school from which he never fully recovered. Regardless, if efforts are not made to realign achievement and ability, the problem is likely to deteriorate further.

In-School Remediation

In some cases, the child may qualify for extra help through an in-school special education or resource program. The guidelines for qualification vary from state to state, but in every instance a significant discrepancy between ability level and skill level is the central requirement.

Remediation can also be obtained by contracting with a private tutor or tutoring group, in which case the extra help is delivered on a one-on-one or small group basis outside of school. In recent years, a number of private tutoring programs have sprung up around the country. Known as learning centers, they provide remedial help in groups of three to five children.

The advantages of having a child receive remedial help from a school-based special education program are:
- The teachers are highly qualified and receive continuing education on a regular basis.
- There is a virtual guarantee of close communication between the special education teacher and the classroom teacher.
- In-school programs are free and convenient.

However, the problem with in-school programs is that a child cannot receive help through them simply because he needs it. Ideally of course, every child should be able to receive a special education tailored to his or her individual strengths and weaknesses, but as things stand, in order to qualify a child for in-school assistance, it must be shown that the child has a disability of some sort. In the absence of mental retardation, severe behavior problems, chronic health problems, or physical handicap, the underachieving child probably won't qualify as learning disabled (LD).

The manner in which public schools use the term *learning disabled* can be highly misleading. The fact that a child qualifies for an LD program does not necessarily mean that the child has a neurological (central nervous system–based) or developmental (maturational) dysfunction that interferes with effective learning. It may simply mean that a significant gap exists between the child's ability and his or her academic achievement and that the gap has not responded to traditional, classroom-based interventions. As I've already said, a discrepancy of this sort justifies remediation but does not necessarily justify attaching the LD diagnosis to the child.

Under the circumstances, even if a child legitimately qualifies for a special education program, I am generally not in favor of securing remediation through the schools. To begin, I don't like the fact that children can't get into these programs without first being labeled, especially when the label is given *for the express purpose of getting the child into the special education program*. And yes, that does happen despite the fact that (a) it is a violation of public education law and (b) schools insist it does not happen.

Second, it's hard to tell just how much progress a child is actually making in a special education program. Once a child is in a program of this sort, report card grades usually improve because the child is being evaluated against lowered academic expectations. The parents see the improved grades and think progress is being made, when in fact it may not be.

I've come across many children who, after several years of part-time work in resource programs, were still well behind in their skills. By the time this fact was brought to light, the majority of these kids had lost so much ground that they could never catch up without being retained. And even if retained, they had lost so much confidence in themselves and so much interest in school that effective academic rehabilitation had become a virtual impossibility.

One might ask, "Why didn't the schools just retain them to begin with?"

That's an interesting question, and one we'll look at in more depth in the next chapter. At this point let's just say that public schools are biased against retention. Private schools are not. This bias means that a child who needs to be retained, whose problems could have been solved much more easily had he been retained, is tested, labeled, given special education services, and moved along from one grade to the next. Meanwhile, his problems do not get any better and probably get worse.

The defenders of these programs claim that these are children who would fall through the cracks in the regular classroom. Ah, but studies have found that children tend to make more rapid progress if they are *not* grouped homogeneously, that is, according to ability. (Note: This finding does not generally apply to children who have IQs lower than 80.)

The last, but not the least, of my objections to these programs is that although the child is receiving remedial help, he's missing whatever instruction is taking place in the regular classroom. For instance, a child may be receiving an hour of remedial work in reading through a resource program, but he is missing an hour of spelling and language arts instruction in the classroom. This policy of robbing Peter to pay Paul cancels whatever benefit the child might be getting from the resource program.

I'm not alone in my opinions and feelings about in-school special education programs and the practice of requiring that children be labeled as handicapped in order to receive special assistance. In late 1989, the National Association of School Psychologists (NASP), a first-rate professional organization with first-order knowledge and influence in this area, released a statement that questioned the practice of requiring that "children be labeled as handicapped and removed from regular classrooms to receive special assistance." NASP called on school systems to take steps to integrate special services and support programs in the regular classroom.

Private Tutors Versus Learning Centers

For all these reasons, I generally recommend that, when needed, remedial help be obtained through private tutors or learning centers. Granted, these options are more expensive and certainly not as convenient, but as things now stand, they involve fewer complications and undesirable side effects than do in-school programs.

Which is generally better, a private tutor or a learning center? Depends on how you look at it. Private tutors are usually less expensive than learning centers simply because they incur less overhead expense. They also work one-on-one with the child, whereas in a learning center, one teacher usually works simultaneously with several children. Instead of providing true remediation, however, many private tutors end up providing nothing more than homework assistance and support. This may help the child keep up in school, but it fails to get to the bottom of the child's problem and is only slightly more helpful than having a parent sit and do homework with the child night after night.

A private tutor usually brings a bit more of a warm personal touch into his or her work with a child than a learning center. If it doesn't overshadow the tasks at hand, that can be extremely motivating. Nevertheless, when contracting with a private tutor, parents need to make their expectations explicit. Make it clear that you are contracting for remediation, not fun and games, and ask the tutor to give you a written plan of what she plans to accomplish with your child, how, and according to what timetable.

If you're going to opt for a private tutor, make sure you find a person who has a proven reputation and is certified to teach at your child's grade level and the subjects under discussion. Ask your child's principal or guidance counselor if they have a list of approved tutors whom they regularly refer to parents.

Learning centers are the more expensive alternative. My experience has been that they are also, in the long run, the most cost-effective. A service-oriented business must produce results in order to stay in business, and that rule applies to a learning center as well as a dry cleaner. As a consequence, most learning centers are truly remedial in philosophy and practice. They don't just help the child keep up. They help him *catch up* in his skills so he can keep up on his own. Furthermore, a reputable learning center will have at its disposal an extensive library of instructional materials, something a private tutor is unlikely to have at her disposal, which means that the staff can adapt far more flexibly to a broad range of learning needs and styles. As with anything else, however, there are good learning centers and there are ones that are not so good. When shopping, look for a center that:

- comes highly recommended by other parents and professionals (e.g., pediatricians, psychologists)
- has been in business more than three years (the usual term of a commercial lease)
- employs teachers who are state-certified and have classroom experience
- guarantees your child will be working with a teacher who is certified to teach at your child's grade level and on the subjects for which he or she needs help

- uses a variety of learning materials, thus enabling adaptation to a broad range of learning styles
- uses computer-assisted instruction as a *supplement* to teacher-based instruction rather than as a primary instructional technique
- retests your child periodically to check his or her progress
- guarantees they will contact and continue to communicate with your child's regular classroom teacher
- promises to keep you regularly posted concerning your child's progress in their program

Questions?

Q *Up until this year, my child attended a private school operated by a local church. We put Robbie there because they claimed that with small classes and an accelerated curriculum, their students were achieving at least one grade level above kids in public school. Robbie went there from kindergarten through third grade and always made nearly straight A's. At that point, we moved to a new community and put him in public school. His fourth-grade teacher called us in for a conference several weeks after school started and told us that Robbie's language arts and math skills were not what they should be and that he would need extra help. In fact, she said that if she had known this before the start of school, she'd have recommended that he repeat the third grade. How can this be?*

A It can be because it takes more than small classes and an accelerated curriculum to get an entire group of children of different ability levels to perform one grade level above public school expectations. It takes an act of God, which even a church-operated school cannot order at will.

Many small private schools make this same claim. They create the illusion of higher achievement levels by beginning academic instruction in kindergarten, focusing on memorization instead of comprehension and concept formation and emphasizing rote drill over exploratory learning experiences. Indeed, they're generally successful at infusing children with lots of facts but not at helping children learn how to synthesize those facts creatively. In reading, word recognition is stressed over passage comprehension. In writing, grammar and punctuation are stressed over creative expression. In arithmetic, facts are stressed over application of concepts.

Obviously, you can't undo what's already been done. Your son needs extra help, and fast! Retention isn't the answer here, and it would probably have created more problems than it solved.

Contract with a reputable private tutor or learning center to work with your son after school. In either case, the tutor or center needs to do a thorough evaluation of your son's academic skills before developing a remedial plan. Before entering into a contract, make sure that the center or tutor has a clear picture of the problem and is able to articulate clear goals along with a concrete set of remedial strategies.

Q **You seem to be saying that there are risks involved in putting children in private school. Are there certain children who *need* private education? If so, how do you identify them? Also, what should parents look for if they're shopping for private schools?**

A I'm not saying that at all. There are no definite, across-the-board risks involved in putting children in private schools. There are very good private schools, and there are ones that wouldn't qualify as even okay.

The better private schools provide an important, worthwhile alternative to public education. Their classrooms are generally smaller, the attention is usually a bit more personalized, the level of communication between teachers and parents is generally better than you find in a public setting, and often they are able to better meet the needs of children whose talents might not be recognized and cultivated in public school.

The first thing parents should remember when shopping for private schooling is that reputable private schools don't make outrageous claims. They don't need to. They don't claim to be the answer for everybody, just an alternative for some. They don't act like they're in competition with public schools, because they're not. They don't claim to be better, just different. In general, the stronger the school's pitch is, the more skeptical parents should be.

Before making a private school decision, make sure:

- The school is accredited by a reputable educational association.
- All teachers are state certified and attend continuing education programs on a regular basis.
- The curriculum matches, but does not necessarily exceed, that found in local public schools.
- A full-time guidance counselor is on staff.
- Community professionals give the school high marks.
- The school is able to provide extra help—again, outside regular classroom hours—to children who need it.

Q *Our son was an excellent student until this year, when he started seventh grade at the local junior high school. Almost immediately, his grades took a nosedive. The problem is, he doesn't seem the least bit concerned. We don't understand how a child who took such pride in making good grades could now* *be so nonchalant about bad ones. If he weren't so popular, we'd think perhaps we were dealing with depression. What's going on, and what should we do?*

A In all likelihood, what's going on is what I call "seventh-grade slump." The transition between elementary school and junior high or what's sometimes called middle school can be extremely problematic for some children. Junior high teachers tend to be more subject oriented than student oriented, students change classes throughout the day, and teachers are less able and, unfortunately, sometimes less willing to give individual attention. All this means that children are suddenly expected to be much more responsible and self-starting than they were just one year before. Add to this the fact that junior high students are typically paying more attention to social standing than academic standing, and you've got the makings of a potential mess.

If your son were less popular, I might suggest the depression hypothesis myself. The paradoxical nature of junior high is such that socially unsuccessful kids quite often become depressed, which results in poor grades, but socially successful kids spend the majority of their time cultivating their social lives, which also results in poor grades. What's a parent to do?

This is probably a simple case of misplaced priorities, in which case it's unlikely that your son needs anything more than for you to light a strong fire underneath him. Chapter 4 contains suggestions that might prove helpful.

Q *Our nine-year-old son was recently tested at school and found to have a learning disability. The school wants Sammy to work with the special education teacher an hour a day, outside the classroom. How do you feel about this?*

A   I recommend that you have an independent psychologist—one with expertise in the area of learning problems—look over the evaluation done by the school and give you a second opinion. This recommendation has nothing whatsoever to do with the quality of evaluations done by school psychologists, because they are generally excellent, but with the criteria public schools use to identify LD children.

In some public school systems, the criteria used to determine whether a child is LD produce occasional false positives—children who aren't truly LD but whose test results qualify them as such. Bureaucratic definitions also fail to catch many truly LD children during their first two years in school, when remedial efforts will be most successful.

Again, these problems have to do with policies, not people. As a group, school psychologists are well-trained, competent professionals, every bit as capable as psychologists in private practice. The difficult dilemma they face is that they must juggle the limitations and policies of the system, their employer, alongside the needs of the children in the system. The majority of school psychologists are doing the best job they can under the circumstances. But the circumstances don't always allow school psychologists to do the job they're capable of doing.

If you see an independent psychologist, and he or she thinks Sammy would benefit from extra help, I'd recommend that you look into getting him the remedial help he needs through a private tutor or learning center rather than through an in-school program. If you choose, for whatever reasons, to let the school remediate, then make sure Sammy isn't going to be pulled out of class during prime instructional time.

Q   *Our six-year-old started first grade this fall. We've noticed that on quite a few papers he's written certain letters backwards. He did this a lot last year, but when we expressed concern about* *it, his kindergarten teacher told us it was nothing to worry about. At the first PTA night this year, we met his first-grade teacher. She also mentioned the reversals, but she told us she thinks Brian is seeing things backward, a symptom of dyslexia. She recommended that we have him tested. At this point, we are thoroughly confused. Do we have something to worry about or not?*

A Yes, I'd say you do have something to worry about, but it's not the fact that Brian reverses his letters. You should worry about his first-grade teacher, who has jumped to a very wrong conclusion. The problem is that her diagnosis, wrong as it is, could be damaging to Brian. There is the very real danger that she will communicate to him her feeling that something is wrong. If this happens, he may lose confidence in himself and develop performance anxiety, which will surely interfere with his learning potential. Research has clearly demonstrated that a teacher's perceptions and expectations can significantly influence a child's behavior, school performance, and even IQ!

The notion that children who make certain letter reversals are seeing things backwards became widespread in the 1970s. Despite the fact that it borders on the absurd, it persists. If these children truly saw things backward, they would forever be walking into walls, in which case a symptom of dyslexia would be a flat, chronically bruised face.

Even if they *did* see letters backward, they would still write them correctly. Think about it. For example, let's say that for a certain child, d's look like b's. When this child went to write a d, therefore, he would write it so that it would look, to him, like a b, which is to say he would write a d. In other words, if there existed children who saw letters backwards, no one would ever know, and the problem would cause these children no difficulties whatsoever.

The truth is that many six-year-olds reverse certain letters. In fact, letter reversals are fairly common in children through age eight. As one might expect, they occur most often with the letters b, d, e, g, j, p, q, s, y, and z. In most of these cases, the visual difference between one letter and the other is subtle and difficult to remember. So a child innocently substitutes d for b and p for q.

An actual reversal, which might occur with e or s, usually happens simply because the child forgot for the moment the direction the letter faces. In addition, some children may have an initial tendency to turn almost all the letters of the alphabet in the same direction.

Regardless of the reason for these reversals and substitutions, they merit no worry. A patient teaching approach will usually correct the problem within a short period of time. The child makes a reversal or substitution, the teacher gently points it out, the child corrects it, and the proper habit slowly but surely develops.

On the other hand, if a big deal is made about the reversals, if the child senses that people are concerned, he could easily become confused, insecure, and anxious about his school performance. The end result could very well be a child with learning problems. That's why it's so important that you resolve this issue with the teacher. If you find that you can't, then do what you must to see that Brian is transferred to another first-grade classroom where there is a teacher who doesn't make mountains out of molehills.

Q *Then what are the tell-tale symptoms of learning disabilities?*

A There are no clear tell-tale symptoms. There are only *indications*. If enough indications are present, it is reasonable to arrive at the conclusion that, yes, the child in question has a learning disability.

A partial list of these indications follows, but please read them with caution! The fact that a child exhibits some of these characteristics doesn't necessarily mean he or she is LD. However, if many or most of the items describe your child, you should have him evaluated by a psychologist who has experience and expertise in the field of learning problems. The earlier the detection, the better the chances the problem can be corrected. All these symptoms assume a child of at least average intelligence.

◆ Capable of average achievement but performing significantly below ability level in most academic subjects

◆ Difficulty understanding and carrying out written or oral directions

◆ General sequencing problems (e.g., difficulty keeping the days of the week or months of the year in order)

◆ Inflexible or disorganized problem-solving attempts, reflecting inadequate trial-and-error skills

◆ Problems with short-term memory (forgetfulness, absent-mindedness)

◆ Asks a lot of unnecessary or self-evident questions

◆ Often misunderstands what people say

◆ Problems with fine motor coordination (e.g., poor handwriting, immature drawings, "all thumbs")

◆ Problems with gross motor coordination (clumsy, "trips over his own feet")

◆ Difficulty organizing ideas and expressing them orally or in writing

◆ Difficulty with phonics (decoding, sequencing, and blending phonetic sounds)

◆ Difficulty with reading comprehension

◆ Easily frustrated by schoolwork, has developed an "I can't" attitude

◆ And finally, what some LD experts have called the most obvious symptom of all: poor spelling skills

I should also mention that a significant number of LD children are also found, upon examination, to have what are called soft signs of neurological (central nervous system) dysfunction, meaning that there are fuzzy indications of slight neurological impairment but no hard-and-fast evidence.

Q *Our eight-year-old son has dyslexia. As a result, he's already more than a year behind in reading skills. We recently watched a talk show featuring a learning disabilities specialist who said most learning disabilities were inherited. Is this true?*

A What the LD specialist said indicates he's not objective when it comes to research, because although some researchers believe there is a hereditary factor, no one has found a genetic smoking gun. Some learning disabilities may be hereditary, but others may be induced in utero by, say, the mother's use or overuse of drugs, tobacco, alcohol, even coffee. Some may result from prematurity, others from inadequate nutrition during infancy and early childhood.

I happen to believe that most—but by no means all—learning disabilities can be explained in developmental terms. In other words, children develop specific learning disabilities as a result of not having had adequate opportunity to exercise certain important skills during their formative years (birth through age six). As a result, these skills fail to adequately strengthen. In school, these maturational deficiencies translate into problems learning to read, write, understand directions, and so on.

Since the early 1960s, learning disabilities have become epidemic among school-age children in America. Many believe this sharp increase has been caused by better identification procedures. I don't. I think we've had to put more effort into research and identification *because* of the increase. Better identification procedures don't *cause* epidemics; they come about as a result of them.

It's interesting to note that learning disabilities are not nearly as much of a problem in European school-age populations as they are in the United States. Since we share much of the same gene pool, this seems to minimize a genetic explanation and suggests that the reason for this country's epidemic may be largely cultural or environmental.

The question then becomes, "What are the most typical differences in upbringing between European and American children?"

There are many, to be sure, but one of the most striking has to do with television. By and large, European children watch very few hours of television a week, and American children watch between twenty-five and thirty. Can large amounts of television cause learning disabilities? Developmental theory strongly suggests it can.

A vast array of skills and talents is contained in the human genetic code. In order to activate this program, the preschool child must be exposed to environments and experiences that promote the exercise of those talents. In other words, the more creatively active the child is during his or her formative preschool years, the more talented he or she will eventually be.

Watching television is a *passivity,* not an activity. It does not properly engage any human potential—motor, intellectual, creative, social, sensory, verbal, or emotional. Therefore, by its very nature, and regardless of the program, television is a *deprivational* experience for the formative-years child.

Reading is not *one* skill but a *collection* of skills. In order to learn to read well, a child must come to the task with the complete set. If certain pieces are missing or damaged, learning to read will be that much more frustrating for the child.

The average American child has watched six thousand hours of television before he enters first grade. Think of it! Can we truly expect that the necessary set of learning skills can endure that amount of developmental deprivation and survive intact?

And let us not forget that so-called learning-disabled children are only the tip of the "Why Can't Johnny Read?" iceberg. Since the mid-1960s, as the amount of television watched by the typical child has soared, scholastic achievement measures have slipped steadily downhill, and the high-school-age illiteracy rate has nearly tripled. And now, complicating matters even further, today's kids have video games and cell phones to contend with.

Could our love affair with more and better electronic devices be lurking behind our national reading crisis? We may never know for sure. The question is, is it worth the risk to ignore the question?

Q *You seem opposed to serving the special needs of learning disabled children during school hours. If I read you correctly, you recommend they remain in regular classrooms and be given individual tutoring after school. Can you be more explicit about this position of yours? As a special education teacher, I reacted defensively to your advice.*

A You read me correctly. But none of what I have to say about so-called pullout (pull the child out of the classroom) programs for LD children discounts the competence and dedication of special education (resource) teachers. In fact, as a group, special education teachers are probably the most well-trained teachers. I simply think their talents are not being used to the best degree possible.

In the first place, to qualify for a pullout program, an otherwise normal child must be identified as LD. I question whether this label does more to clarify or confuse, help or hinder our understanding of these children and their needs. The fact is, a wide range of individual differences exist among LD children—too wide a range, in my estimation, to justify grouping them under one banner. The fact is these children are performing significantly below what measures of their ability would predict. To catch up, they're going to need more individual attention than a classroom teacher can provide. Why this fetish with labels when the facts will do?

Furthermore, policy in most school systems is such that once a child qualifies for and is placed in a resource program, he or she cannot be held back a grade (retained). In my career, I've had considerable experience working with such children. My finding has been that retention is often the most effective way of responding to their problems.

I also question the manner in which pullout programs are often marketed. Parents tell me (and I've heard) many school administrators and teachers claim these programs help children catch up, in other words, that they bring performance levels up to par with ability. In general, however, the needs of these children all but demand that material be presented at a slower speed and with more repetition than would be the case in a regular classroom. So, I ask, how can a child catch up when the curriculum is slowed down? My experience has generally confirmed that they don't.

These claims seem even more suspect when one considers that the special education teacher may be serving as many as eight children at any given time. This allows for more individualization, but in many cases it's not enough.

Finally, pulling a child out of the regular classroom often robs Peter to pay Paul. For example, if a child is pulled out during spelling instruction to receive extra help in math, then math skills may improve while spelling skills suffer.

For all these reasons, I recommend that if parents can afford it, they contract for one-on-one tutoring outside of school hours. Meanwhile, school systems need to develop better means of helping these children. After all, that is their responsibility.

Q *Our eight-year-old son, a third grader, was recently tested because of reading difficulties and found to be dyslexic. According to the tests, Robby's IQ is well above average, but his reading skills are slightly below par. In addition, he still reverses certain letters and sometimes whole words. When we asked for an explanation, we were told he has a neurological disorder that causes certain perceptual problems. We were also told that many famous, successful people have or had dyslexia, including Thomas Edison. Can you elaborate?*

A Dyslexia is a diagnostic label often applied to children whose reading skills are lagging significantly behind ability, as measured by a standard IQ test. According to a Yale Medical School study, most youngsters classified as dyslexic in grade one no longer qualify for the diagnosis by grade three.

This suggests that rather than being a distinct neurological disorder, dyslexia is simply part of the continuum of normal reading ability, or it's just a label certain people use when they don't know how else to explain something. Actually—and my saying this always gets me in trouble with the dyslexia crowd— no one has proven that dyslexia involves a congenital neurological dysfunction. Yale Medical School's findings suggest that it is not.

To propose the existence of dyslexia or any other learning disability on the basis of a disparity between reading skills and a score on a so-called IQ test assumes these tests are infallible, which they aren't. The subject of continuing professional controversy, their predictive value is questionable, along with their validity. An accurate presentation of findings would leave parents with the understanding that although these tests are the best indicators currently available, it isn't possible to base hard-and-fast conclusions on them. Besides, a gap between apparent ability and reading level could be caused by low motivation, a lack of opportunity, a home in which reading is not modeled or encouraged, inadequate instruction, or family problems.

It would be more factual to simply say, "Compared with other children his age, Robby's reading skills are slightly below par. He seems to possess the ability but may need some individual attention to properly engage that ability." But people make money from labels. Common sense is not a cash cow.

It's important to keep in mind that all discussions of dyslexia are theoretical. No one will ever be able to prove that Thomas Edison or any other historical figure had dyslexia, whatever dyslexia is. How does one ascertain that a dead person had a disease that has no physical correlates?

Until someone demonstrates conclusive, concrete proof of a neurological malfunction underlying the problems of so-called dyslexic children, I propose nothing more radical than that we stick to the facts.

Q *Our sixteen-year-old daughter was struggling with algebra, so we got her a tutor. She has a part-time job. Do you think she should pay for all or part of the tutoring?*

A The most creative approach to this issue was shared with me by parents who required that their child (also a high school student with a part-time job) pay for her own tutoring. But if her grades improved, the parents reimbursed her. Needless to say, the grades improved. The principle is simple: One takes more responsibility for that which is not free.

6

The Case for Retention

It used to be called failing or flunking. It is now called retention or nonpromotion. In any case, it's the practice of having a child repeat a particular grade in school. These days, any discussion of the subject must also include the issue of delaying an age-appropriate child's entrance into kindergarten.

The use of retention was first associated with the introduction of graded schools in the nineteenth century and developed in response to the problem of students who seemed ill equipped to move successfully on to the next grade level. Concern about the possible negative effects of holding children back was first expressed in the 1930s; nevertheless, retention continued to be fairly common and widespread.

Beginning in the 1960s, retention became less used as schools sought alternative ways of managing children with academic problems. Concerns about the psychological and academic effects of holding children back were a major factor in the development of special education programs, which were virtually nonexistent until the mid-1960s. At present, a disproportionate amount of education funding is consumed by special education programs (as a function of the number of special education students relative to the total public school population).

Today, a child who struggles academically in a public school setting is more likely to be considered a candidate for special education than a candidate for retention. Once a child is identified as a special education student, it would take an act of Congress to retain him. From that point on, the child is moved from grade to grade regardless of progress. Academic standards for the child are lowered to such an extent that his grades become essentially meaningless. He can be in the fifth grade, doing third grade work, and receiving mostly B's on both his daily work and his report card. Furthermore, by the time this all-too-typical special education student reaches high school, he has fallen further and further behind his classmates. In effect, he is incentivized to drop out. In this regard, it is significant to note that the dropout rate for special education students is *twice* that of the general high school population.

In a nutshell, that is why I am a proponent of retention. I believe that if this *typical* special education student (i.e., he has no measurable disabilities but was performing significantly below grade level when identified) had been retained instead of assigned a label and special education status, the possibility of his dropping out would be much lower. The statistics certainly support this theory, as does common sense.

The major barrier to retention in public schools is money. When a child is retained, it costs the system money. The child must now be educated for an additional year. When a child is given special education status, the system qualifies for additional funding. Therefore, I contend that in many (but not all) cases, the decision to assign a child to special education is less in the interest of the child than of the system. In short, public schools are economically incentivized to put as many children as possible into special education programs.

For the most part, private schools do not have this incentive. In fact, private schools are economically incentivized to retain, which they are most likely to recommend early on. The way most private schools retain is through delayed kindergarten entrance, hence the increase in the number of five-year-olds in private school prekindergarten programs. To me, that makes perfect sense. It does mean that the private school in question is making more money off those students, but it greatly increases the likelihood that every student in first grade will be working at or close to grade level. In other words, it's a win–win outcome (school–child), whereas public school policy often results in win–lose.

More children are retained in kindergarten than in any other grade. In just six years from 1979 to 1985, the number of children repeating kindergarten increased nearly 60 percent. Most kindergarten-retained children are either chronologically young when they enter school—so-called late-birthday children—or, regardless of birth date, they exhibit slight maturational shortcomings at the end of their first kindergarten year. Among advocates, and I am one, the general feeling is that an extra year in kindergarten gives these children time to catch up in developmental skills before they start first grade, thus reducing the risk of later school failure and thus lowering the dropout rate.

Once upon a time not so long ago, most educators agreed that retaining a child in one of the early elementary grades (K–3), kindergarten in particular, wasn't a psychological issue; rather, it was a developmental concern. Early retention gives the immature child an additional year to catch up. Furthermore, because the material is already familiar, retention gives an immature child the opportunity to experience academic success on the second go-round. This positive experience forms the foundation for continued school achievement.

Early retention of this sort has come under heavy fire of late from many educators, and the ensuing debate has inspired some strong language. Commenting on the finding in one study that kindergarten-retained children had more academic, social, and emotional problems later than did a comparable group of children who had been promoted to first grade, a well-known educator pronounced, "Keeping kids back in kindergarten is immoral."

If that's the case, then I know plenty of immoral kindergarten teachers. Not long ago, a Long Beach, California, teacher wrote me a long confessional in which she admitted to having retained seven—that's right, *seven*—late-birthday children in one year. She wrote, "I asked them if they would like to stay with me another year, and they all said they would. They were of at least average intelligence. Their only 'handicap' was their late birthdays. Their parents were in favor of the decision to retain. The next year, the children all had a wonderful kindergarten experience and were ready and eager for first grade. As you might imagine, I am in total favor of retention in certain cases, and I know seven happy children who can back up my opinion!"

To this teacher's testimonial, I can add my own. I've had a hand in retaining more than a few kindergarten children. Without exception, those children benefited from a second year in kindergarten. I'm quite sure that if they had been moved prematurely to first grade, many of those same kids would have fallen further and further behind, would eventually have been placed in special education programs, and might never have realized their potential.

As for the notion that retention increases the likelihood of emotional problems, one should keep in mind that most social science research is done by people who are trying to prove something. Taking the retention issue as an example, the researchers in question are trying to prove that retaining a child increases the likelihood that he or she will develop persistent feelings of failure. That means their research is contaminated by their preexisting bias. They design a study that is likely to yield the conclusion they're seeking and interpret their data in like fashion.

One of my grandchildren repeated kindergarten. At the end of his first kindergarten year, his kindergarten teacher recommended that he be retained (his birthday is in late summer). When his parents asked my opinion, I told them that his teacher knew best. They retained him, and he eventually became an honors student.

Another statistic supporting early retention is the fact that students in the 1950s and early 1960s—when retention was the norm for students who were struggling academically—did better in school than have post-1960s kids. Their achievement levels were much higher at every grade, and the high school dropout rate was much lower.

I once evaluated a kindergarten child who was having problems associated with some slight developmental delays. It was late in the year, the teacher had recommended retention, and the parents wanted my opinion. The results of my evaluation convinced me that the little boy would not be ready for first grade in the fall. I concurred with the teacher's recommendation. Nonetheless, the parents went ahead and advanced him to the first grade. Six weeks into the year, they called to tell me that the first-grade teacher had already talked with them about having their son tested to determine his eligibility for special services.

"What do we do now?" they asked.

Unfortunately, because these parents had not taken my original advice, they were between a rock and a hard place. Since their son had already started first grade and looked forward to going to school, we were past the point of putting him back in kindergarten. I didn't want to see him labeled and put in a special education program, especially in light of the fact that his problems would probably have resolved themselves had he been retained. After much discussion among all concerned, the less-than-satisfactory decision was made to let him stay in first grade but retain him at the end of the year. This fiasco points up the kinds of problems that can occur when a child should be retained but isn't.

In the opinion of some experts, the K–3 curriculum in most American public schools is developmentally inappropriate for large numbers of children. In many kindergartens, children are receiving instruction that was once reserved for first grade, creating inappropriate demands on their growth and development when they are unprepared to cope with these new expectations. Thus, their chances for failure are increased dramatically.

Recognizing that change takes place slowly within the educational bureaucracy, we need to create educational options that will facilitate success for young children whose readiness level is not yet suited to the demands of the accelerated curriculum. One researcher calls these alternatives—delayed kindergarten enrollment, developmental pre-K programs for four-year-olds and five-year-olds with late birthdays, and transitional programs between kindergarten and first grade—"gift-of-time options."

All of these alternatives, specifically intended to provide immature children with early success experiences, work better than retention. But if retention is the only option, experience has taught that the earlier it takes place, the better. One study conducted in California compared children retained in kindergarten with those whose parents declined the recommendation and sent them directly on to first grade. A follow-up evaluation found significantly higher achievement levels persisting through grade three for the retained group. Another study of more than six hundred children in Minnesota found that both self-concept and achievement were significantly lower among children for whom a growth year was recommended and *not* taken.

A third study compared children who entered school when they were chronologically young (their birthdays occur in June, July, August, or September) with children who were older at school entrance. The findings demonstrate that:

- Chronologically older children in a grade tend to receive more above-average grades than do younger children in the same grade.
- Older children are much more likely to score in the above-average range on standardized achievement tests.

- The younger children in a grade are more likely to eventually be labeled learning disabled than older students in the same grade.
- The early academic problems frequently experienced by late-birthday, or summer children, often follow them throughout their school careers and sometimes even into adulthood.

For these reasons, it is generally recommended that summer children be given one of the three gift-of-time options already mentioned. On the other hand, if a child's developmental unreadiness is not detected in time, and early retention becomes necessary, parents must present that decision to the child in terms that are not only positive but also self-incriminating. For example, parents might say to a child, "We made a mistake. We started you in school too early, before you were ready. Repeating [the grade in question] will give you a chance to catch up with yourself, so that learning can be more fun and easier for you."

The only (slight) disagreement I have with this position concerns delayed kindergarten enrollment. If a child is eligible for kindergarten, even if he has a late birthday or some obvious but minor immaturity, and the kindergarten is developmental rather than academic, I say enroll him. A tremendous amount of maturation can and does take place that year. Even without special attention, kindergarten children who are somewhat behind can, and do, catch up. For that reason, I prefer giving the child the benefit of the doubt.

I've been party to many instances when retention—even when it occurred late—proved extremely helpful. My experience tells me that it's more appropriate for certain academically troubled students than for others. Unfortunately, retention is often used as an expedient when other intervention options might well have solved the child's academic problems. The proper question is, "For what children and under what conditions is retention most likely to be successful?" In this regard, I find that retention stands the greatest chance of working when:

- It's done during the early elementary years (K–3).
- The child is significantly behind in developmental or academic skills, and individual tutoring (prescriptive education) is no longer a realistic option.
- Factors other than ability are the cause of the child's academic difficulties.
- Other therapeutic and remedial interventions are used in conjunction with retention to address those difficulties. This recognizes that retention never solves a child's problems; it only provides a context in which those problems can be solved.

Under these circumstances, I find that retention can result in considerable benefit to a child, assuming it is handled supportively and positively by both the child's parents and the teacher. Needless to say, if a child is made to feel that retention is punishment for doing poorly in school, it isn't going to work.

Almost all rules have their exceptions, and the following story illustrates one such example. A number of years ago, the parents of a sixth-grade boy asked my advice about problems their son was having in school. He was small for his age and obviously self-conscious and defensive about his size. He had difficulties getting along with other children, his classroom behavior was often disruptive, and he'd fallen nearly two years behind in his academic development.

My evaluation indicated that he had the ability to do above-average work in school. In all likelihood, a combination of factors had snowballed to throw him off track. He was probably an appropriate candidate for retention in kindergarten or first grade, but if his difficulties had been identified and addressed early enough, that might not have been necessary. However, all that was water over the dam. The question now was how to best help him at this stage of the game.

After careful consideration of all the options, I recommended that he be retained in the sixth grade and given remedial help outside school. My decision turned on the fact that seventh grade meant a move to junior high school, where he'd be changing classes throughout the day. Furthermore, junior high school teachers tend to be more subject- than student-oriented. Under the circumstances, I feared that this young fellow's problems would only become more difficult to correct if he took them with him into seventh grade. Not only was he not mature enough to accept the responsibility expected at that level, he didn't have the skills to do the work. He would have needed remedial classes or more extra help than was realistically possible to provide.

Knowing that we were running a risk and hoping to minimize it, I coached the parents about not only when and how to break the news to their son but also how to respond supportively to his anger and anxieties. As we expected, he reacted badly. He ranted and raved and even threatened to run away. The parents were patient but firm. They accepted his feelings, were as reassuring as possible, and let his reaction run its course.

The next year, even though he came to school with a chip on his shoulder, the boy quickly discovered that his size was no longer a disadvantage in a younger group. He made friends quickly and became a leader both inside and outside the classroom. Furthermore, the fact that the work was familiar, combined with the extra help he was getting outside school, made it easy for him to make good grades. He began taking pride in his work, and his classroom behavior improved commensurately. The parents later told me that he had just completed his junior year in high school, was popular with his classmates, and was an A student as well. His mother said, "Being retained in the sixth grade was the best thing that ever happened to him."

The key ingredients in this youngster's successful retention were timing, parental support, and academic remediation. One thing is certain: To simply retain a child and do nothing to address the problems that contributed to the child's academic difficulties is irresponsible and will, in the long run, create more problems than it solves.

There is a widespread belief, even among professionals, that the retained child will forever see himself as a failure and sink slowly but inexorably to the level of that internal expectation. Frog feathers! If you want to help a child who's falling behind in school develop a disabling attitude toward himself, you need only continue promoting him from grade to grade. To create the illusion that he's being helped, have him tested and placed in a program where he receives special attention outside the regular classroom for a short time each day. Instead of protecting a child from feelings of failure, these manipulations virtually guarantee them, as evidenced by the higher dropout rate for special education students.

My finding, based on forty-plus years of accumulated experience, is that a child who should have been retained in one of the early grades but wasn't is likely to fall further and further behind his age-mates as the years march on. Eventually, overwhelmed by frustration and feelings of defeat, the child gives up altogether. He becomes apathetic toward school and often develops behavior problems. He finally succeeds in alienating himself not only from the system but also from most of his peers, and he contents himself with the easy company of other peripheral students. In all likelihood, this youngster will become an in-school dropout before age sixteen and an actual dropout shortly thereafter.

The news that he or she is going to be retained is initially upsetting to a child (especially those in third grade or higher), but with adequate adult support the upset is usually short-lived. As Dr. Louise Bates Ames, former associate director of the Gesell Institute of Human Development at Yale University, said, "Even if it is traumatic to keep them back, it's better to traumatize them once and get it over with than to have them face problems every day for the next twelve years."

When I recommend retention, it is always in conjunction with other remedial approaches, including individualized prescriptive education (tutoring, covered in Chapter 5), motivational strategies (see Chapter 4), and teaching parents the do's and don'ts of effective homework management (Chapters 2 and 3). Note the conspicuous absence of counseling for the retained child. Although many clinicians think counseling is necessary to soften the impact of retention, I have *never* found it to be necessary and believe that it can be counterproductive. If you treat a child as if he *ought* to be psychologically damaged by having been retained, you run the risk of setting a self-fulfilling prophecy in motion. You can create a problem where there would have been none at all or prolong a problem that would have otherwise run its course in a short time.

Many psychologists, social workers, and guidance counselors are so wedded to the belief that the right sort of counseling can solve any problem they fail to realize that the retained child may hear this message in the counseling process: "You have a right to feel bad about what's happening to you." The child would certainly not be able to articulate this perception, but it would have the effect of increasing the child's resistance to the retention and therefore negatively predisposing its outcome. My experience is that it's far more advantageous to teach the child's parents how to inform him or her of the decision to retain, acquaint them with the range of reactions possible (denial, sorrow, anger, blaming), which closely resemble the grieving process, and coach them on effective ways of responding to those behaviors.

Questions?

Q *Our son is a late-birthday kid. He's scheduled to start kindergarten this fall, but the program in our schools has a fairly heavy academic emphasis, especially during the second half of the year. If I take your advice and keep him out of school a year,* *is it going to make much difference whether I keep him at home or put him in a nonacademic preschool program?*

A I think it could make a big difference. There are several advantages to putting him in a nonacademic preschool program. First, because he'd be with a group of children his age, he'd make more gains in social and play skills than he would if he were simply at home. Second, because most of the activities would be structured and teacher directed, preschool would prepare him better for the expectations his kindergarten teacher will have. Third, a nonacademic program incorporates activities that stimulate and strengthen specific developmental skills. Therefore, it's likely that he'll make more progress in such a program than he would at home.

There are a number of helpful things you can be doing with him at home. You can read to him at least thirty minutes a day. You can provide paints, crayons, and colored pencils for him to draw and color with. You can take him on nature walks and educational walks through various parts of the town you live in. You can prepare him for the responsibility of school by giving him a routine of chores to do around the home. And that's just for starters. His preschool teacher will be able to give you even more suggestions.

Q *Our son started kindergarten in September and turned five in October, only a few days before the deadline. Here it is November, and his teacher is already talking about having him repeat. It seems he isn't quite as mature as the rest of the kids, which is understandable, and that he isn't progressing as fast in his skills. How can we handle this without doing damage to his self-concept?*

A It's a bit early to be making final decisions about who's going on to first grade and who isn't, but let's say you and the teacher eventually decide to have your son repeat. Will that mean you made a mistake by putting him in kindergarten this year? Hardly.

Your son will spend the year productively, advancing in his social skills and being introduced to entry-level academic structures. The alternatives would have been to either keep him at home or put him in a preschool program for four- and young five-year-olds. Given that the kindergarten curriculum is developmental rather than academic, there isn't anything a developmental preschool could have done that kindergarten isn't doing. This way, there's at least a *chance* he'll be ready to go on to first grade on schedule.

Your son will handle the idea of spending another year in kindergarten as well as you handle it. If you act like there's something wrong, he'll think there's something wrong. On the other hand, if you act like nothing's wrong, like spending a second year in the great and wonderful kindergarten place is no more significant than crossing the street, he'll shrug his shoulders and get on with it.

If the decision to retain is made, there's no need to give it a big, dramatic buildup. When the year is almost over, his teacher should sit down with him and explain that since he's younger than the rest of the kids, she wants him to stay with her another year. And next year, since he'll be one of the oldest and will already know a lot about kindergarten, he can be a big help to her and the other kids. Won't that be just spiffy?

And he'll come home and tell you the good news, and you'll be happy for him, and that will be that. On the outside chance that he is upset, just reassure him it's for the best and things are going to be fine. If he sees that you're confident in the decision, he'll believe you. Trust is a powerfully good medicine.

Q *We recently applied for our son, age five, to attend kindergarten at a private elementary school in our community. After giving* *him a readiness test, they informed us that his academic skills are not up to their standards—he doesn't yet know his letters and numbers, for instance—and his fine motor coordination is slightly delayed. They even suggested he might have a learning disability. Even though they acknowledged he was bright, they said their program was not set up for the kinds of problems he might possibly experience in school. We left the interview feeling devastated. Does this sound serious to you? If so, where do we go from here?*

A First, I am generally opposed to readiness testing with this age child, primarily because a child's developmental skills are still in formation at this age. That raises doubts about the reliability of these tests and, therefore, any conclusions drawn from them.

A number of factors can contaminate a child's performance on a readiness test, including lack of familiarity with testing procedures, not understanding why the test is being given, and inadequate rapport with the examiner. Under the circumstances, there's a good chance that readiness testing will do nothing more than set off unwarranted false alarms. For that reason, they should be used conservatively, only by qualified professionals, and interpreted cautiously, with respect for their inherent limitations and drawbacks. If a readiness evaluation raises serious concerns about a child's developmental integrity, a more comprehensive evaluation should be done before final decisions are made.

Second, there is absolutely no substance to the popular notion that children should come to kindergarten already equipped with certain basic academic skills, including letter and number recognition and the ability to write their names. Recent research indicates that it is not only inappropriate to apply these sorts of expectations at the preschool level but also potentially damaging. A premature attempt to push these skills can create problems that would not have developed otherwise. A number of experts believe we are creating some learning disabilities by pushing literacy at children too early and too hard.

In this regard, it's interesting to note that in the 1950s and before, most children came to first grade not yet reading, and many didn't even know their ABCs, yours truly included. And by today's standards, elementary classrooms in the 1950s were *criminally* overcrowded. Yet those children outperformed post-1960s children at every grade, and that continues to be the case. Unfortunately, the only parents today who can completely ignore the pressure to teach academic skills to children younger than five are those who homeschool, which is a good reason to do so.

The fact that a five-year-old child falls below the norm with respect to the emergence of one or two developmental skills is not anything to get excited about. If you looked hard enough, you could probably find delays of one sort or another with the majority of children this age, especially boys. As I've already said, time and proper developmental programming are the great equalizers in situations of this sort. One year of developmentally appropriate kindergarten has helped many an immature child resolve these sorts of problems.

Where do you go from here? Look into other kindergarten options—private, public, church-supported—in your community. Put your child in the program that puts least emphasis on academics. Or consider homeschooling (Chapter 8).

Q *I'm a first-grade teacher who takes exception to your opinion that kindergartens should be developmental rather than academic. The real push for children of kindergarten age to learn to read comes from the fact that first graders are expected to attain a certain standard of accomplishment. If children do nothing but play for one year in a kindergarten setting, it's a real chore to accomplish the goals set for them in first grade.*

A   First, the guided play activities typical of developmental kindergartens are not a waste of time, as your objection implies. They are creative, playful means of activating, exercising, and strengthening all the perceptual, motor, and cognitive skills children will need to become good readers. Developmental psychologists such as David Elkind, the author of numerous books on this issue (e.g., *The Power of Play*), have long recognized that play is the most productive of all early childhood experiences.

Your remarks also imply that the child should be made to conform to the timetable rather than the timetable to the child. So if the system decides children should have acquired a certain level of proficiency in reading by the end of first grade and this level can't be achieved unless instruction begins in kindergarten, then instruction begins in kindergarten. Such is the price children are paying for schools being afflicted with achievement-test-score neurosis.

Second, teaching first-grade children to read will be a chore only if the system establishes unreasonable, unnecessary, and unrealistic goals. But that is exactly what school systems tend to do when they become more interested in improving their rank in the national achievement scores contest than they are in meeting the needs of the children they are supposedly serving.

Your attitude, unfortunately common among today's educators, is a perfect example of the reasoning behind the notion that the younger a child reads, the better. In general, Americans have a habit of judging the merit of things on the basis of product or outcome and ignoring the *process* by which that outcome is attained. This is particularly the case when it comes to evaluating things that directly affect children, things like television and organized sports and early academics. In the latter case, it is a fact that kindergarten-age children can be taught to read. But the fact that it *can* be done does not necessarily mean that it *should* be done.

Jean Piaget, the eminent Swiss developmental psychologist, once spent a summer at Harvard studying with Jerome Bruner, the eminent American developmental psychologist. As Piaget was about to board a ship for his return to Europe, a reporter asked his opinion of Bruner's contention that given proper instruction, any child could be taught any skill at virtually any age.

Piaget replied, "Only an American would think so."

Q *So what should parents be doing during the preschool years to help their children eventually become successful readers?*

A To begin with, parents need to realize that reading is not just one skill but the interplay of many:

- *Inquiry:* Reading is, first and foremost, an act of inquiry, exploration, and discovery. An inquisitive toddler rummages through drawers and cabinets in search of knowledge. In the same way, and for the same reasons, an inquisitive ten-year-old rummages through the pages of a book. Contrary to current mythology, learning to read is easy, assuming the child comes to the task equipped with the developmental tools needed to perform it.

- *Imagination:* Reading ignites the imagination. A seven-year-old reader transforms words into images in much the same way a three-year-old transforms an old shoebox into a sailing ship. Imagination is essential to reading comprehension. It breathes life into the static word, making it dynamic. Without imagination, words are hollow. The child who has misplaced his imagination (or had it *displaced* by such things as watching too much television) will see reading as a chore rather than a joy.

- *Coordination:* Reading involves the coordination of perceptual, mental, and physical processes—eyes, brain, and hands. The eyes scan lines of print and transmit raw data to the brain. The brain processes the data, decoding and retrieving information stored in its vast data banks, making associations, and forming mental images, thus arriving at the "Ah-ha!" of understanding. Meanwhile, hands hold the book, turn the pages, and adjust the depth of field so the eyes can focus.

◆ *Self-concept:* Like any other meaningful activity, reading offers the child a challenge. "He has a good self-concept" is really a roundabout way of saying, "He likes to be challenged." Like every other challenge, reading offers a child the opportunity to grow in self-reliance and responsibility.

A successful reader, therefore, is an inquisitive, imaginative, well-coordinated child who enjoys being challenged. There are three fundamental things parents *should* do to build these solid foundations.

First, parents should provide safe, stimulating environments that encourage inquiry and exploration. From his earliest months, if a child's inquiries into the world are rewarding (as opposed to frustrating), and if parents feed (as opposed to deprive) his appetite for discovery, when the appropriate time comes he will want to rummage as eagerly through books as he did through drawers and cabinets when he was younger.

Second, parents should spend lots of time reading to children. And read with gusto! Breathe life into the story. Make the child's eyes grow wide with wonder at the power of the printed word. Few things are more completely enriching to a child—emotionally, socially, and intellectually—than being read to. Nestled securely in his parents' arms, listening to them paint word-pictures, a child learns that reading feels good. When the time comes, he will want to recreate this feeling for himself.

Third, parents should read—a lot. Children follow the examples set by their parents. If parents read, children will, in all likelihood, follow suit. On the other hand, if parents rely on the television as a primary source of entertainment and information, so will their children.

Then, there are two things parents *should not* do if they want their children to become successful readers.

First, they should not teach a preschool child such things as the alphabet and how to read unless the child specifically asks to be taught. Even then, take a casual approach, and if the child loses interest, leave well enough alone. Studies have repeatedly demonstrated that the head start produced by preschool reading programs lasts only a few years.

Second, parents should not let preschool children watch more than a few (that's three!) hours of television a week, if any. Increasingly, researchers are finding that children who spend disproportionate amounts of time watching television during their formative years have more reading problems than children who watch very little. A child watching television is not exercising *any* of the skills he or she will eventually need in order to become a successful reader. Experts are now saying that this lack of appropriate developmental exercise and stimulation, accumulated during hours and hours of television watching, can permanently impair a child's reading ability.

Q *My friend and I both have three-year-old boys who will enter four-year-old kindergarten this fall. I'm concerned because her son knows how to write his name and can identify lots of colors and even all fifty states. His parents are now working with him on the names of the state capitals, which he's picking up on fairly quickly. My son can't write his name yet and shows no interest at all in memorizing anything. Do I have cause to worry?*

A Worry about what? You have something to worry about if your son:

- ◆ Can't converse fairly well and clearly
- ◆ Shows no interest in playing with other children
- ◆ Regularly messes himself
- ◆ Can't occupy himself independently and creatively
- ◆ Sits for long periods of time staring at the wall
- ◆ Throws wild tantrums during which he bangs his head on hard objects

But the fact that he doesn't write his name and perform what are nothing more than mnemonic tricks on command is no cause whatsoever for concern.

With due respect to your well-intentioned friends, who are probably convinced their pet human is gifted, any three-year-old possessing average intelligence whose parents invest the time can be taught to write his name, correctly identify all fifty states, and so on. A young child's mind, uncluttered as it is, can absorb all sorts of irrelevant junk. It's truly too bad that some parents are so eager to be seen (and to see themselves) as superior to the rest of us that they waste their young children's precious time in these ways.

The fourth year of life is for learning how to play with others, learning proper manners, and spending independent time inquiring, imagining, and creating. To force a three-year-old to do tedious and completely irrelevant memory drills is brain abuse, pure and simple, even if these exercises are conducted as games.

Let me assure you, when both of these children are in their teens, no one will be able to tell which one knew the names of all fifty states when he was three. However, I venture to predict that your son will be the happier of the two.

I asked a recent audience, "How many of you entered first grade not able to correctly identify all twenty-six letters of the alphabet?"

Lots of hands went up, and let me assure readers that this audience had not been bused in from a local rehabilitation center for adult illiterates. In fact, it was composed entirely of people who worked for a large high-tech corporation.

Later, several managers told me the best potential employee was not necessarily one who'd made the best grades in school but rather one who was creative, resourceful, and industrious and required little direct supervision. Those attributes are learned during the third and fourth years of life.

Furthermore, evidence suggests that occupying this child's time with rote exercises—even teaching him or her to read— may be counterproductive. One study found that teaching a child to read during his preschool years increased the likelihood he wouldn't enjoy reading as a teen.

So if you've been obsessing about the possibility that your son is behind the preschool performance curve, you can stop. By showing no interest in memory drills, he's telling you he's a happy, well-adjusted three-year-old who's not the least bit interested in performing at dinner parties. In this case, the child knows best.

CHAPTER

7

When to Medicate

A chapter with this same title was included in the 1990 version of this book. At the time, I was on the fence about the diagnosis of attention deficit–hyperactivity disorder and the use of medication to (supposedly) treat it. I believed there was some validity to the diagnosis and circumstances that justified the use of medication to treat ADHD behaviors. I was wrong.

Shortly after the publication of that first version, I began to realize that people in what I now call the ADHD Establishment—including pharmaceutical company bigwigs and most but not all psychologists, psychiatrists, and pediatricians—had absolutely no concrete evidence to support their claims about this supposed behavior disorder. They still don't.

They claim, for example, that ADHD is caused by differences in the brain, but their own research fails to find significant brain differences in most children diagnosed with ADHD. Furthermore, they cannot prove that such a brain difference—if it is ever determined, beyond doubt, to be characteristic of *all* children diagnosed with ADHD, thus proving the disease theory—is the cause or the effect of ADHD behaviors.

The human brain changes in response to long-standing repetitive behaviors of any sort. Professional baseball pitchers, if compared with the general population, would undoubtedly be found to have brain differences, and the same can be said of many other highly specialized professions. By the reasoning of the ADHD Establishment, those brain differences caused them to become pitchers. No, the repetitive behaviors required of professional baseball pitchers caused the brain differences. Similarly, the behaviors that define ADHD are by definition repetitive. If they weren't, the diagnosis wouldn't exist. When a person with ADHD behavior is found to have brain differences—and remember, these differences are not true of every person so diagnosed or even a substantial majority of them—the likely explanation is the same as the explanation for professional baseball players: The behaviors themselves, over time, caused the brain differences.

This is not the case with a verifiable physical disorder. Take epilepsy, for example. Every single person diagnosed with epilepsy has verifiable brain differences. Epilepsy usually has its onset during infancy or early childhood, too early in life to theorize that seizures caused the brain differences. It's clearly the other way around: The brain differences cause the seizures associated with epilepsy. Therefore, epilepsy is a verifiable physical disorder. ADHD is not. Period.

The ADHD Establishment claims that ADHD is associated with what they call biochemical imbalances. They make that claim for every psychiatric diagnosis, by the way. Most people think that because doctors and other people who have impressive capital letters after their names use the term *biochemical imbalance*, it must be a real thing. But it's not. It's a theoretical thing, and no one has ever been able to verify that a person's biochemistry is out of balance. In fact, for reasons that are not important to this book, such a theoretical imbalance *cannot* be verified, ever. A leading psychiatrist has even admitted that the term is nothing more than a "useful metaphor." That means it's not real. It's a myth. The ADHD Establishment knows this, yet they continue to tell parents that their children behave the way they do because of biochemical imbalances. They don't say "We *think* ADHD *may* be caused by a biochemical imbalance" or "It *may* be that your child's behaviors are caused by a biochemical imbalance." They speak unequivocally, as if they are telling the truth. They aren't. Period.

The ADHD Establishment claims that ADHD behaviors— impulsivity, short attention span, problems finishing tasks, problems waiting one's turn, interrupting conversations, low tolerance for frustration, to mention a few—are inherited. To prove that a child has inherited certain behaviors, one must prove that the same behaviors were characteristic of the child's parents, aunts and uncles, and perhaps grandparents. There is no evidence that significant numbers of children raised before 1970 came to school displaying the behaviors associated with what is now called ADHD. Women who taught elementary school in the 1960s and before consistently, without exception, have told me they did not see children with ADHD behaviors when they were teaching. The inherited theory is hogwash. Period.

The ADHD Establishment claims that the medications they prescribe for treating ADHD work. But they also know that none of these medications has ever reliably outperformed placebos in double-blind clinical trials. Brace yourself, because *no psychiatric drug has ever reliably outperformed placebos in double-blind clinical trials.* A double-blind trial is one in which neither the person dispensing the pill nor the person taking it knows whether the pill is a real medicine or a placebo like bicarbonate of soda. I said all this (and a lot more) at a conference in 2012. When I was finished, a gentleman in the audience stood up and introduced himself as the director of research at a major pharmaceutical company. He said, "Everything John is saying about psychiatric drugs, including ADHD medications, is true. It is the pharmaceutical industry's dirty little secret." He then admitted he had just put his job in jeopardy and asked that what he had just said not leave the room. In effect, the drugs in question are expensive placebos. A parent may say, "My child took [an expensive ADHD medication], and his behavior and school performance greatly improved," but the empirical evidence suggests that the child might have improved just as much if he'd taken a sugar pill.

Furthermore, ADHD drugs do not *cure* ADHD. If and when they appear to work, all they do is suppress symptoms for four to eight hours. Then the symptoms return. Yet the people who prescribe these drugs keep prescribing them, claiming they work. But in the final analysis, the ADHD Establishment isn't interested in curing ADHD. It's making them entirely too much money—more money, in fact, than any psychiatric diagnosis ever has. They intend to just keep on treating it and pretending that the new medications they come up with are better than the old ones. But the new ones don't do anything more than suppress symptoms for four to eight hours. How, then, are they better? They aren't. And they don't work. They are a pharmaceutical treadmill. Period.

The vast number of children being identified as having ADHD is largely accounted for by school referrals to community professionals who specialize in its diagnosis and various (largely bogus) treatments. As I explained in Chapter 6, public schools are financially incentivized to qualify children for special education services. Private schools are incentivized by the fact that children on ADHD medication tend to perform better on achievement tests and present fewer behavior problems. In both cases, the diagnostic bar is being continually lowered, the result being ever-increasing numbers of kids being referred, diagnosed, and put on medication. In my estimation, based on many years of experience, most of these kids' problems can and should be dealt with using nonmedical interventions. The following two stories will illustrate that.

Changing Schools Cures ADHD!

Shortly after a nine-year-old boy enters a certain very expensive private school in Alabama, his third-grade teacher begins complaining to his parents that he is unfocused in class. She recommends that he be tested for ADHD by a local psychologist. The boy's mother subsequently discovers that by the fifth grade, 65 percent of the kids at this school have been diagnosed with ADHD and are taking medication. The parents asked my advice.

I point out that even if one were to accept the validity of an ADHD diagnosis, the above statistic is absurd. The school was a den of diagnosis working in cahoots with a local professional who operated what I call an ADHD factory. One red flag in this regard was the school's recommendation that the boy be tested for ADHD. In the *Diagnostic and Statistical Manual,* eighteen diagnostic criteria are listed for ADHD. Nine of the eighteen must be characteristic of the child in question in order to assign the diagnosis. Not one of the criteria references a test result. All eighteen criteria are descriptions of behavior. ADHD specialists give expensive batteries of tests for one primary reason: to create the impression that something scientific is being done to arrive at the diagnosis. And believe me, these specialists absolutely know that regardless of the test results, they are going to diagnose ADHD.

Once a private school with this record says a child has ADHD, then they are going to continue berating the child's parents until they cave in. They may even sabotage the child's education in order to make their case. If the parents stand their ground, the school is ultimately going to tell them to take their child elsewhere. In short, no good could come of this situation. In the meantime, the quality of this boy's educational experience was in jeopardy. I told the parents to get him out of there, fast!

The parents took the bull by the horns and moved their son to a public school. Eight weeks later, his mother sent me a follow-up note that included an account of his report card. She wrote: "It was perfect! All A's in every academic category and Satisfactory in every behavioral category, even in neatness. This is the same child who, at the private school, got consistently bad evaluations for his behavior. For the first time in his life he says that he loves school. He came home last week nearly floating in enthusiasm and pride because his teacher had cited him as a role model for other children for his dedication to his work and his behavior in class."

But the most fascinating part comes next. Mom continues, "You may also be interested to know that, prior to consulting with you, I had gone ahead and had my son tested by a very well-regarded psychologist here in our hometown. I was outraged with his recommendations, which were that my son be given medication for a neurological disorder and placed in a remedial school for ADHD children. The tests were obviously geared to arrive at a diagnosis of ADHD, and sure enough, that's what came up."

Fancy that! A nine-year-old is diagnosed with ADHD. His parents object to both the diagnosis and the school's management of him, so they move him to another school, and just like that, his ADHD is cured. In that case the notion that ADHD is a disorder that stems from inborn neurological problems goes out the window. You simply cannot cure a brain-based disorder by putting the afflicted child in a different school.

ADHD Cured by Locking Child Out of His Room!

A certain young man was a major behavior problem both in school and at home. He was disruptive, disrespectful, and disobedient. His fifth-grade teacher, principal, counselor, and the school psychologist repeatedly suggested that the young man had ADHD. These well-intentioned folks reassured the boy's parents that ADHD is genetic; therefore, his behavior wasn't their fault. He needed medication to help him control the impulses he could not control otherwise. The parents resisted this well-intentioned hogwash.

"Finally," the mother told me, "we reached the limit of our tolerance for his shenanigans. He came home from school one day to discover a padlock on the door to his bedroom, which houses his television, computer, video game unit, sports equipment, models, and so on. We told him he'd be allowed in his room for fifteen minutes in the morning to dress for school and fifteen minutes in the evening to get ready for bed, which was going to be seven-thirty every night, seven nights a week. His bed was going to be the sofa in the living room—most comfortable, if you ask me."

The boy was stunned. When he threatened to report his parents for child abuse, they reminded him that they intended to take proper care of him in every way. "But go right ahead," they said. "Tell whomever you like how abused you are."

This would last at least six weeks, they told him. During this time, he would not be allowed to participate in any after-school activity, have friends over, use the phone, watch television, or go anywhere except to accompany his parents. Furthermore, every single incident of misbehavior at school or home would add a week to his exile, and no amount of good behavior would shorten it.

"It was amazing," his mother said. "His teacher called us several days later to tell us he'd become a completely different child. She'd never seen so much improvement so quickly. He became a model child at home as well—polite, cooperative, talkative, a general pleasure to be around."

Six weeks later, the padlock was removed from his door with assurances it would be reattached at the first hint of a relapse. It never had to be used again.

With more parents like that, the makers of anti-ADHD drugs might have to go into the sleeper-sofa business.

The Diseasing of America's Children

In 2009, pediatrician DuBose Ravenel—an emeritus consultant to Dr. James Dobson—and I published *The Diseasing of America's Children* (Thomas Nelson, Nashville) in which we laid out all the above facts, and more. We said ADHD is a farce and that the people who specialize in its diagnosis and "treatment" are scamming parents. We proposed a theory that explains the post-1960s ADHD epidemic and gave actual solutions that have cured the problem for many, many children.

My licensing board—the North Carolina Psychology Board (NCPB)—keeps a sharp eye on me. I'm a rebel. I rock the psychology boat. I don't promote the psychological party line, especially concerning ADHD and other childhood behavior diagnoses. If I make an unsupportable claim in one of my books or in my weekly newspaper column, the NCPB will surely hear about it, and I will be summoned to appear before them to defend myself against charges of misleading the public. I've been saying this heretical stuff about ADHD for a long time now. No one in the ADHD Establishment has ever complained to the NCPB. The reason is simple: If I were subjected to a psychological trial, the facts about ADHD would have to be made public. They don't want the facts made public. So they leave me alone, hoping I'll just go away.

One more thing: Some people think I'm merely saying that ADHD is overdiagnosed. No, that's not what I think. I see no good reason to believe that the supposedly brain-and-biochemistry-based disorder called ADHD even exists. It's a chimera. But it's a chimera that makes a lot of people a lot of money. For that reason and no other, it will be with us for a long time.

If you want a more in-depth analysis of this fascinating subject, read *The Diseasing of America's Children*. In closing, however, the title of this chapter asks the question of when one should medicate an otherwise normal kid who exhibits behaviors associated with ADHD. My one-word answer: Never.

8

What About Homeschooling?

I am a proponent of homeschooling. (And by the way, that does not mean that I am opposed to public or private education. There are good and bad schools in both categories.) I am a regular speaker at homeschool conferences and have served on the board of a national organization that defends the right of parents to direct their children's education. Nonetheless, I do not think homeschooling is appropriate for every child. Nor do I think that all parents are equally suited to homeschool. It is not enough that parents may disagree with the philosophy and methods of the public and private schools in their community. That may be the least important justification for homeschooling. The decision to homeschool should take a number of variables into consideration, including the child's suitability, the emotional and organizational fitness of the parent who will be doing the homeschooling, and the availability (or lack) of a homeschooling parent support network. It may seem obvious, but it is vitally important that both parents are on board with the decision to homeschool. It's an almost-certain recipe for failure when, for example, the husband is telling the wife he wants the children homeschooled, but she is reluctant.

Obviously, homeschooling requires a significant time commitment on the part of the parent who will be in charge of the process. That's the first question to be answered if you're considering homeschooling: Do you have the time? A mom who is already juggling numerous commitments may find that the requirements of homeschooling push her over the stress cliff. Although they do not by any stretch constitute a majority, there are numerous examples of successful homeschools where both parents work outside the home. It can be done, but only if both parents are equally committed to making it work.

Then there's the question of the state of the mother–child relationship. Has she clearly established her authority over her children? Do her children do what she tells them to do, or do they push back— whine, refuse, ignore, argue—when she gives them instructions? Are her children accustomed, by the time they reach school age, to completing tasks for her on a daily basis? A mother who began assigning her children household chores when they were three years old has more effectively trained them to properly respond to her in the role of teacher than has a mother who did not.

Obviously, the behavior of the child in question is an important consideration. It is a decidedly bad idea for a mother to attempt homeschooling with a child who has not accepted her authority. Unresolved discipline problems will pollute the homeschooling process. They need to be resolved before the mother takes this leap of faith. Here's one homeschooling mom's testimony:

> *We were homeschooling and having trouble with our oldest basically not doing what we told him to, be it homeschool assignments or stuff at home. Establishing leadership and*

authority in all areas for me made it all work together. Once the kids realized they had to listen and obey instructions, whether it was a math assignment or doing the dishes, every part of family life has been better. Prior to hearing you talk, I had wondered if homeschooling was the issue, and if I should send him to school to solve the problems. But that would not have solved anything, because he still would have come home and ignored my instructions. I actually think it might have made things worse, as he was already not respecting us, so throw that attitude of "I can do whatever I want and I can get my own way if I whine enough" into a mix where negative influences are certainly available, and who knows where it would have gone.

Is there an existing local homeschooling moms' cooperative that the mother can plug into for support? My experience tells me that the optimal homeschooling situation is one in which the child would be getting some course content from other mothers (or listening to a coach, Sunday school teacher, or music teacher). It's certainly advantageous if the homeschooled child learns to adjust as part of a group rather than having everything individualized to him or her. This set of circumstances also increases the accountability of each child and mother in the homeschool group.

If you're considering homeschooling your children, I recommend the following:

- Contact your state and local homeschooling associations for recommendations concerning curriculum materials and for a referral to other homeschooling moms in your immediate area.
- Talk to other homeschooling moms about their experience, their assessments of the pros and cons, and their take on the various curricula that now abound in the homeschool marketplace. Moms whose children are several years older and

have been homeschooling for a while and moms of multiple children can be especially helpful. If a mom homeschools only one child, she tends to think all children should react the same way. Once you homeschool more than one child, you realize that different personalities come into play. For example, homeschooling boys versus girls is a very different experience.

◆ Join a homeschooling moms' co-op.

◆ Attend a homeschool conference such as those put on by Great Homeschool Conventions (www.greathomeschool-conventions.com). Connect with other homeschool parents and families, visit the many vendor booths, attend the educational presentations. Absorb as much information as you can. The more you familiarize yourself with homeschool culture and the many resources that are now available to homeschooling parents, the better.

For the mom who is considering homeschooling but is unsure of her ability to do so successfully, there are virtual schools that tend to be a middle-of-the-road experience. Because the lesson plans are laid out and some of the curriculum is delivered online, a virtual school involves more managing than teaching. It is a great place to start because it allows parents to have the benefits of homeschooling—learning at home, knowing what the children are learning, increased time with family and for other activities, the ability to go at your child's pace (faster or slower than the typical classroom)—but without the burden of having to create the entire curriculum. Despite the name, virtual schools do not generally involve that much time in front of a computer, but through an online hookup, the homeschooling mom can receive support upon request from teachers, help with testing, and so on.

Questions?

Q *I homeschool my two children, ages seven and nine. The class day lasts from eight-thirty in the morning until two o'clock in the afternoon, after which they usually do homework for an hour or two. During that time, they are constantly coming to me, asking me to go over material we've already gone over during school. This is preventing me from getting my own work done. What should I do?*

A You should tell them that after two o'clock you are no longer their teacher; you're their mother, and you don't intend to re-teach material you taught during school. If they were attending regular school they wouldn't have access to their teachers after school. Likewise, in your homeschooling situation, they shouldn't be able to have teacher on demand after school hours. As things stand, they know they don't have to give you their full attention during the school day, so the effectiveness of home-schooling is reduced and your stress level is increased.

This is a mother–child boundaries issue, as are many if not most contemporary parenting problems. Instead of being in control at any given time, you are either mother or teacher; you're allowing your children to make that determination. In any relationship, clearly defined boundaries are essential to mutual respect. Without those boundaries, one party will begin to take advantage of the other. In this case, your kids are not being consciously manipulative; they're simply doing what you're allowing them to do.

The solution to this problem is for you to establish clear definitions of what your children can and cannot expect from Mom after school. Limit the number of school-related questions you will answer after two o'clock to two per child. Tell them that after they've finished as much of their homework as they can, each of them can bring you two questions, but you'll spend no more than ten minutes answering them. After the ten minutes, they're on their own.

I guarantee that if you enforce this dispassionately, your kids will pay better attention during school hours and eventually all but stop asking after-school questions. And you'll be able to get your mom-work done. Independence in a parent–child relationship is always a mutual thing.

Q *My five-year-old son is an only child whom I homeschool. He talks back, argues, and generally wears me down. I need help getting him to realize that no is no, that I mean what I say. I know I'm the problem. Help!*

A Better that you have come to grips now with the fact that you are the problem than when he's much older, and these difficulties have acquired much more momentum. Before giving you some advice, I must repeat: I do not recommend homeschooling when the child in question is disobedient, disrespectful, and generally difficult to control. Preexisting discipline problems are counterproductive to an effective homeschool environment. Discipline problems should be solved before homeschooling is attempted. So the first recommendation I'm going to tender for your consideration is that you send your son to regular school until you get his behavior under control. Be clear on this: Sending your son to school will not solve the problem, but it will give you time to solve it before you begin homeschooling again.

Today's parents believe discipline is a technology involving the manipulation of reward and punishment. In other words, they believe discipline is accomplished through the proper use of consequences. The fact is that whereas consequences are sometimes needed and more with some kids than others, the proper discipline of a child is primarily a matter of using authoritative speech, including authoritative body language. Taking one example, do not (as the majority of parenting pundits advise) get down to your child's level when you speak to him or her. In so doing, you look like you are pleading. Stand upright. When I speak on proper discipline, I emphasize the need for parents to act like Superior Beings. It may come as a surprise, but contrary to the parent–child egalitarianism parenting "experts" have promoted for more than a generation, adults are superior to children.

Learn to use what I call leadership speech when giving instructions and communicating decisions. Use the fewest words possible, come straight to the point, and do not give explanations. Explanations sound persuasive as opposed to authoritative. Therefore, they invite argument.

Wrong way: (The parent is scrunched down, hands on knees.) "Honey, it would really help Mommy if you'd pick up the toys in the living room and put them away so my friend Susan and I can use that room to talk and have coffee without a lot of distractions. Will you do that for Mommy, okay?"

A child is likely to say to an instruction communicated in that wimpy fashion, "I was here first! Why do I have to move? And you never let me have anything to drink in here! No!" Mind you, the parent has created the problem. The child is only responding to the parent's non-authoritative presentation.

Right way: (The parent is standing upright.) "I need you to pick up these toys and move them to another room. I'll be back in a few minutes to see that it's done." (And then, walk away. Standing there will invite resistance.)

As you're walking away, if the child asks, "Why?" stop, turn around, and say, "Because I said so. Any other questions?" And then leave the scene.

Someone is bound to ask, what if the parent comes back in the room and the toys aren't picked up? Ah! Now a consequence is called for. But proper leadership speech will reduce the need for consequences by at least 50 percent within a month. First, stop repeating yourself. Give your child any instruction once, and once only. Second, pick the toys up yourself. Say nothing. Just pick them up. And then, immediately after dinner that evening, inform the child that he's going to bed. He is, after all, too tired to pick up his toys when told.

When it comes to consequences, be consistent, but do not be predictable. Be full of surprises!

Q *You've often said that parents should not be involved with their children but rather should establish a clear boundary in the parent–child relationship. I agree in principle, but as a home-schooling mom, I have no choice but to be highly involved with my kids. Can you help me resolve this conflict?*

A In any relationship, it's essential to respect boundaries. One of the stumbling blocks in contemporary parenting culture is the general lack of a clear boundary between parent and child. The symptoms include the so-called family bed, married couples who are more involved with their children than they are with one another (in terms of attention paid, time spent with, interest shown, and so on), and families that are organized around children's activities. The underlying problem is that today's parents are more concerned about being liked than respected by their kids.

This social fashion is by no means confined to the parent–child relationship. The need to be liked by children has infected the teaching profession (in some school systems students actually rate teachers on likability), and it manifests itself more generally in such imprudent things as adults wanting children—even very young ones—to call them by their first names.

To your question, homeschooling does not, should not, require a high level of involvement between parent and child. The best homeschool curricula facilitate a considerable amount of independence on the part of the student and foster a clear boundary between parent-as-teacher and child-as-student. The recognition is implicit that effective teaching requires just such a boundary. An excess of parent involvement in homeschooling is also known as micromanagement, and unfortunately, many and perhaps even the majority of homeschooling moms are guilty of it. Micromanagement in any context breeds communication problems if not conflict and lowers the motivation of the people being micromanaged. In that regard, it is significant to note that when homeschooling moms seek my help for difficulties with their kids, they always describe communication problems, conflict, and lack of motivation.

Most homeschool curriculum reviews rate the package on parental involvement (high, medium, or low). I recommend low. I do not mean, however, that the lower the level of parent involvement, the better. One homeschooling mom who always chooses low-involvement curricula said this to me:

> One of the things that I enjoy about homeschooling is the read-alouds or projects we all do together as a family. That is higher involvement than just handing out individual assignments to each child, but our children have strong relationships partially due to the time we spend together, so some involvement is a good thing!

In the 1950s, the effectiveness of American public education peaked. Never before or since has student achievement been so high. That's also true of the teacher–pupil ratio, which was approximately one teacher per thirty-five students at the elementary level. My first-grade class, for example, consisted of fifty students and one teacher. She had no aide. Teachers did it all by themselves back then. No student received much individual attention. And yet, from first grade on, we baby boomers outperformed today's kids at every grade level. And most of us came to first grade not knowing our ABCs!

The 1950s teacher taught a given subject for fifteen to thirty minutes, gave a class assignment, and retired to her desk to grade papers or just glare at us. When the time was up, we exchanged papers, graded them, and handed them in. Then the teacher moved on to the next subject module, which she handled pretty much the same way: teach, assign, grade, then move on. That's the perfect teaching paradigm for homeschooling moms. It's a low-involvement model that puts most of the responsibility on the student, which is where it should be.

The most effective homeschooling generally takes place in the context of a collaborative effort on the part of two or more homeschooling parents, each of whom accepts certain teaching responsibilities, and the children are usually involved in extracurricular activities (e.g., sports, band, clubs) through the local public school system. The notion that the isolation of homeschooling is antithetical to learning to deal with real life is belied by the consistent finding that kids who've been homeschooled score as well or better than their peers on measures of social adjustment. Nonetheless, a mix of activities is good. A homeschool co-op will provide some of that, but all homeschooling parents should keep in mind that they can put their kids into public school programs, sports, and other activities. Homeschooling parents are still taxpayers!

Parents often ask me what I think about homeschooling, to which I reply, "For whom?" In other words, homeschooling is by no means a one-size-fits-all option. It should not be embarked upon without considerable forethought, investigation, and conversation with other homeschooling parents. Some parents are suited to it; others are not. In any case, selecting an appropriate curriculum is key to the overall success of the endeavor.

Q *We have fairly significant, ongoing behavior problems with our six-year-old son and have tried various disciplinary approaches with little positive result. The latest problem involves the fact that I homeschool him. He isn't at all motivated to work for me, although he was never a problem last year in kindergarten. The work is on his level, and I have beautiful and interesting hands-on Montessori materials for him to work with. Nonetheless, the problems are nearly constant. Today, for example, he ended up in his room by 10:00 in the morning, allowed to have only books and no screen time for the rest of the week. I punished him for complaining, lying down (saying he was tired), not following directions, and generally goofing off. Am I on the right page here?*

A It gives me no pleasure to tell you that no, you are not on the right page. The fact that your son didn't give his kindergarten teacher any problems last year tells me that you and your husband have created the problems you are observing. You obviously have not succeeded at establishing your authority over your son. The problem is further compounded by an approach to discipline that is consequence-based.

Authority is a certain attitude, a certain presentation. For a parent to *act* like an authority figure, he must first *think* like an authority figure, meaning he must possess complete confidence in the legitimacy of his authority. The first step in that direction is for the parent to fully embrace the incontrovertible fact that adults are superior to children. I call it acting like a Superior Being. The fact is, most parents do not act like Superior Beings. They act like peers. Instead of using an authoritative voice when they speak to their kids, they use a pleading, persuasive voice. They feel the need to explain themselves. When they give instructions, they get down to their children's level (which most parenting experts recommend) as if they were talking peer-to-peer.

That's the problem in contemporary parenting. That sort of obsequious approach to one's child puts the child in charge. Behavior problems are the logical outcome, and those problems are not going to be solved by punitive consequences.

I strongly recommend that you read my book *The Well-Behaved Child: Discipline That Really Works!* (Thomas Nelson, Nashville, 2010) in which I explain how to institute effective authority (the attitude) and use consequences properly. A proper authoritative attitude significantly reduces the need for consequences. Similarly, when a parent is using lots of consequences, and especially when, as in your case, they're not working, I absolutely know the right attitude is lacking.

Until you get these problems under control, put your child back in regular school. Under the circumstances, homeschooling is counterproductive. If you decide, against my advice, that you're going to continue homeschooling, I suggest that you find and join a homeschool cooperative. The likelihood is—and his experience in kindergarten bolsters my view—he'll be more cooperative with other mothers than he will be for you.

Q *I have homeschooled my now sixth-grade daughter on and off through elementary school. This school year, I homeschooled her until October, at which time she said she wanted to go to real school again. Now she says she hates school (it's boring and she struggles with math) and wants me to homeschool her again. I've figured out that the conflict over homeschooling versus real schooling has to do with the fact that all of her friends attend real school, and she's very social. Do you think I should take her out and homeschool her again?*

A Up until now, you've obviously been letting your daughter decide when you homeschool her and when she attends so-called real school. The question that you need to answer for yourself is, "Where my daughter's education is concerned, who knows better, me or her?" For what it's worth, I'll answer the question for you: You know better. You've already told me that her decisions are based primarily on emotional factors: School is boring, her friends are there, math is frustrating, and so on. When a decision of this magnitude is based on one person's feelings and the person is a child, the decision is not going to be in the child's best interest. If you want to solicit her feelings, that's fine, but you should make the decision, and if your decision doesn't match her feelings, so be it. At the very least, I would have her sign a contract in which she agrees to be homeschooled for a minimum period of time before any changes will be considered.

Q *Several of my friends who homeschool maintain that homeschooling keeps children away from bad influences within the peer group and other inappropriate situations at school. Is it realistic to keep a child sheltered from such things? How are they going to know how to function in the real world? Also, doesn't homeschooling necessitate overinvolvement on the part of the mother?*

A Homeschooling and sheltering are hardly synonymous. A parent shelters by preventing a child from encountering realities that would be helpful, not harmful, to the child. For example, a parent who helps her third-grade child with his homework every night, making sure he answers every question correctly, is sheltering. She is preventing her child from learning that he is capable of meeting challenges on his own. With good intent, she is all but guaranteeing that he will have serious problems when he begins to encounter challenges she cannot help him through. After all, in the real world you don't have anyone sitting with you, making sure you don't make mistakes.

"But John!" a reader might be exclaiming. "The homeschooling mom is sitting with her child, too!"

That simply goes to show that you can't judge a book by its cover. The mother in the above example is enabling, thus disabling. If she is following one of many homeschool curricula, the homeschooling mom is not creating a dependency; rather, she is facilitating independence in learning.

Many moms whose children attend institutional schools spend more time on a daily basis helping their children with homework than the typical homeschooling mom spends on direct teaching. Make no mistake about it, however; some parents who homeschool have no business doing so. They are unqualified or are doing so for all the wrong reasons.

A joke found on the Internet: The parent of a homeschooled child says, "My wife and I used to worry about our child's socialization, but now we make sure he can relate to his peers. We let him watch R-rated movies."

Along those same lines, a public school teacher recently told a friend of mine who is a homeschooling mother that her child needed "a few hard knocks by other children to toughen her up." My friend calmly replied, "I don't want my child to be tough."

We tend to forget that until the twentieth century, most children were homeschooled. Some of the Founding Fathers, for example, were homeschooled. No evidence exists that when the time came, they had difficulty dealing with reality. Homeschooling has proven itself, both historically and in recent times. Because of the homeschool explosion of the last twenty years, a good amount of data on homeschooling outcomes now exists and continues to accumulate. The evidence is clear and irrefutable: Homeschooled children suffer no disadvantage, academically or socially, over institutionally schooled children. In fact, when matched demographically with children who attend institutional schools, homeschooled children do better on measures of achievement, behavior, and social skills.

Family psychologist John Rosemond is director of the Center for Affirmative Parenting, headquartered in Gastonia, North Carolina. CAP is a national resource center that provides parents with practical parenting advice and materials. Toward that end, CAP conducts workshops and educational presentations for parents and professionals who work with children. CAP also has available print, audio, and audiovisual materials on parenting and child development.

Since 1978, John has written a nationally syndicated family column that currently appears in more than one hundred newspapers across the United States and Canada. His columns have appeared regularly in *Better Homes and Gardens* magazine and *Hemispheres*, United Airlines's in-flight magazine.

Throughout the year, John is in demand as a public speaker. His humorous, provocative parenting presentations and workshops have drawn consistently high marks from parent and professional groups all over the country.

Last, but by no means least, John is husband to Willie and father to Eric and Amy, both of whom are married with, between them, seven children. Eric is a corporate pilot. Amy is a homemaker.

Those interested in obtaining information about John's presentations, workshops, or parenting materials can do so by going to his Web site at www.rosemond.com.

Portions of this book were previously published in the author's book *Ending the Homework Hassle* (Andrews McMeel, 1990).

Andrews McMeel Publishing, LLC
an Andrews McMeel Universal company
1130 Walnut Street, Kansas City, Missouri 64106

www.andrewsmcmeel.com

14 15 16 17 18 MLT 10 9 8 7 6 5 4 3 2 1

ISBN: 978-1-4494-2230-1

Library of Congress Control Number: 2014936196

ATTENTION: SCHOOLS AND BUSINESSES
Andrews McMeel books are available at quantity discounts with bulk purchase for educational, business, or sales promotional use. For information, please e-mail the Andrews McMeel Publishing Special Sales Department: specialsales@amuniversal.com